SALT AND LIGHT

SALT AND LIGHT

Talks and Writings on the Sermon on the Mount

by

Eberhard Arnold

PLOUGH PUBLISHING HOUSE
Hutterian Society of Brothers
Rifton, New York

© 1967, 1977 by the Plough Publishing House of
The Woodcrest Service Committee, Inc.
Hutterian Society of Brothers
Rifton, NY 12471

Edited and translated from the German by
the Hutterian Society of Brothers
Rifton, New York

First edition   1967
Second edition, paperback   1977

Library of Congress Cataloging in Publication Data

Arnold, Eberhard, 1883–1935.
    Salt and light.

    1. Sermon on the Mount. I. Title.
[BT380.A7   1977]   226'.9'06   77–1204
ISBN 0–87486–170–5

Printed at the Plough Press
Hutterian Society of Brothers
Farmington, PA, USA

CONTENTS

ACKNOWLEDGMENTS

The text of Chapters Five, Six, and Seven of the Gospel of Matthew at the beginning of this book is from the *Revised Standard Version of the Bible*, copyrighted 1946 and 1952 by the Division of Christian Education of the National Council of Churches, and used by permission.

The verses quoted at the end of *How Can Men Fight Mammon?* (Letter of James, 5. 1-7) are from *The New English Bible, New Testament.* © The Delegates of the Oxford University Press and The Syndics of the Cambridge University Press, 1961. Reprinted by permission.

All other Bible quotations in this book, mostly very short, are translated from the German as quoted freely by Eberhard Arnold in his talks or writings.

INTRODUCTION

My father, Eberhard Arnold, was born in Königsberg, East Prussia, on July 26, 1883. Some years later, his father became Professor of Church History at the University of Breslau. His mother, née Elisabeth Voigt, came from a family of scholars.

At the age of sixteen Eberhard Arnold went through a deep experience of conversion. Twenty years later, he wrote that Jesus had called him at this turning point in his life and had chosen him to be a servant and witness to Him and promised to protect him in this service.

So from the beginning he gave witness with his life to what God had shown him and what he had seen: he was to open men's eyes and help them to turn away from the darkness toward the light, away from the power of Satan toward God, so as to receive forgiveness of sins through faith.

From that time on Eberhard Arnold lived

only for his one Lord, Jesus Christ; it was particularly the sharpest words and demands in the New Testament that burned in his heart. He tried even at this early age to lead a radical life of discipleship. Belonging to a privileged upper-class family distressed him. He felt extremely unhappy whenever his parents gave parties. On one occasion he went to his father and said, "Jesus says that when you give a feast, you should invite the sick, the lame, and the blind— those who cannot repay you. For what is special about inviting those who are able to return your invitation?" Eberhard's father was furious and confined him to his room.

Eberhard began to speak at public meetings when he was still in high school and continued in college and as a member of the German Christian Student Union (DCSV).

On Good Friday 1907, he became engaged to Emmy von Hollander and married her in December 1909. She, too, wanted a life of radical discipleship of Jesus. On Easter Sunday 1907, Eberhard Arnold wrote to his future bride, Emmy: "I am so *very* glad that you too love so much to see *Jesus* always in the center. That alone is healthy Christianity. Not teaching, but *Jesus;* not feelings, but *Jesus;* not effort, but

Jesus! Always, nothing but His will, His peace, and His power!"

At this time he was concerned with the question of baptism of faith. He searched through early Christian and 16th century Anabaptist documents. The great number of martyrs among the Baptizers, especially among the Brothers whom men call Hutterian, or Hutterites, made a profoundly shaking impression on him.

In 1915 (during the First World War) Eberhard Arnold was called to Berlin by the German Christian Student Union as the Union's secretary and shortly thereafter as literary director of the *Furche* Publishing House, which still exists today but was then in its early stages of development.

Toward the end of the First World War and in the restless post-war months, the Sermon on the Mount burned particularly on my father's heart. He was able to share the deep impression Jesus' words had made on him in a circle of Christian students who met on the *Frauenberg* (Marburg, Germany) in 1919 for a Whitsun conference of the DCSV. In the words of his student listeners: "Suddenly we pricked up our ears when Eberhard Arnold began to speak about the Sermon on the Mount." They were all so deeply moved that they asked, "Is this the Sermon on the Mount we heard about in our confirmation classes and in our university lectures? Isn't this something totally new?"

A report about the DCSV Conference at Marburg, published by Erwin Wissman in *Die Furche* (1918–1919, pp. 375 ff.) reads as follows:

> The focus of all that was said and thought was Jesus' Sermon on the Mount. Eberhard Arnold burned it into our hearts with a passionate spirituality, hammered it into our wills with prophetic power and the tremendous mobile force of his whole personality. This was the Sermon on the Mount in the full force of its impact, in its absolute and undiminished relevance, its unconditional absoluteness. Here there was no compromise. Whoever wants to belong to this Kingdom must give himself wholly and go through with it to the last! To be a Christian means to live the life of Christ. We are obligated by a burning challenge: the rousing summons to live, and the ominous warning, "He that takes the sword shall perish by the sword."
>
> It is our responsibility to see to it that the one, final revolution of the Spirit really begins . . . that in the Spirit of Jesus we do

His deeds, helping our fellowmen in soul, spirit, and body. There is no other way for us Christians to live in the present age as emissaries of God's Kingdom and pioneers of Christ's rule, which is the only feasible, indeed the only political system we need.

Eberhard Arnold himself writes about the 1919 Whitsun conference in *Das Neue Werk* (1922/1923 p. 104):

Freedom from tradition and taking to heart the sharpness of Jesus in all questions of life, private or public, set the tone of those meetings. Never before had a gathering begun in just that way with folk roundels and the Sermon on the Mount! Discussions centered around simple trust in God's intervention and the working of His Spirit, man's intimate relationship with God's creation, the question of rejecting personal privileges and the use of force, fellowship among men, joy in nature—all of these seen together as a whole. The joy felt by all was deepened by the serious injunctions of the Sermon on the Mount. What made a lasting impression was that through the New Testament Christ himself spoke on the *Frauenberg* just as He had done that very first time in His Sermon on the Mount:

> He was the same Christ who was crucified, who rose again, and sent His life-giving Spirit into a death-ridden mankind.

During this time Eberhard Arnold came very close to religious Socialism because the Churches did so little for the outward need of men. In later years he said that the words of the Sermon on the Mount were concerning him day and night. For him the Sermon on the Mount was not a code of new laws or commands—it was power, light, salt, the City on the Hill.

Eberhard and Emmy Arnold wanted to go the way of discipleship and in 1920 began to live in complete community, without any property, without any possessions, in complete faith in Jesus on the basis of the Sermon on the Mount. Emmy Arnold's sister Else von Hollander was one of those who shared the struggles of the early years with them. The community had an open door for people to come and for people to leave. All kinds of guests came: students, university professors, workers, tramps—people of various nationalities: English, Dutch, Swiss, American, French, and Swedish.

It was a deep joy for Eberhard Arnold and the little community to find out that Hutterian communities stemming from the radical Anabaptist Movement of the 16th century still existed in North America. In 1930 Eberhard Arnold traveled to the United States and Canada to visit the Brothers for almost a year. Through him the German Bruderhof became completely united with them, and he was ordained a Servant of the Word by their Elders.

When Hitler came to power in Germany in 1933, the community came under heavy pressure. At the end of October of that year Eberhard Arnold suffered a serious fracture of his leg. That made his Service very difficult. However, he would not allow himself to be prevented from doing his Service, risking his life to do it.

During those last years of his life he revised his book *Inner Land: A Guide into the Heart and Soul of the Bible*. This greatly enlarged edition was published after his untimely death.[1]

My father, Eberhard Arnold, died on November 22, 1935, under the threat of a shaking world catastrophe and an approaching world

---

[1] Eberhard Arnold *Innenland, Ein Wegweiser in die Seele der Bibel und in den Kampf um die Wirklichkeit*, 1936. English translation, *Inner Land: A Guide into the Heart and Soul of the Bible* (Rifton, NY: Plough Publishing House, 1975). Both editions can be obtained at the Hutterian Society of Brothers, Rifton, NY 12471 USA.

war. He had had to undergo surgery in Darmstadt for his fractured leg, which had never healed properly, and he died immediately afterwards. The loss of this man of God was and still is very shaking for our Bruderhof communities and for all who knew and loved him.

In 1937 the Bruderhof in Germany was dissolved by the Gestapo, expropriated, and declared to be "hostile to the nation." At the time German, English, Swedish, and Swiss members were living there. They all had to leave the country, and since the community had a branch in the Principality of Liechtenstein (founded in 1934), some moved there. The majority, however, moved to England via Holland. A year later all members united in England. During the Second World War the greater part of the community emigrated to South America.

Today the community continues in England and in the United States under the name "Hutterian Society of Brothers." The Bruderhofs continue to live in complete community of goods and try to go the way of Jesus as radically as their predecessor Eberhard Arnold.

November 22, 1976   *Heini Arnold*

Anyone who wants more insight into our common life will be welcome to visit us if he is open and seeking. We offer our guests a chance to share in the community life and work side by side with us. We neither charge guests for accommodation nor pay them for their work.

Because of the number of guests who come to us, please write in advance if you wish to visit one of our communities of the Hutterian Society of Brothers:

Woodcrest, Rifton, New York 12471
New Meadow Run, Farmington, Pennsylvania 15437
Deer Spring, Norfolk, Connecticut 06058
Darvell, Robertsbridge, Sussex, England TN32 5DR

MATTHEW'S ACCOUNT
OF
THE SERMON ON THE MOUNT

Seeing the crowds, he went up on the mountain, and when he sat down his disciples came to him. And he opened his mouth and taught them, saying:

"Blessed are the poor in spirit, for theirs is the kingdom of heaven.

"Blessed are those who mourn, for they shall be comforted.

"Blessed are the meek, for they shall inherit the earth.

"Blessed are those who hunger and thirst for righteousness, for they shall be satisfied.

"Blessed are the merciful, for they shall obtain mercy.

"Blessed are the pure in heart, for they shall see God.

"Blessed are the peacemakers, for they shall be called sons of God.

"Blessed are those who are persecuted for righteousness' sake, for theirs is the kingdom of heaven.

"Blessed are you when men revile you and persecute you and utter all kinds of evil against you falsely on my account. Rejoice and be glad, for your reward is great in heaven, for so men persecuted the prophets who were before you.

"You are the salt of the earth; but if salt has lost its taste, how shall its saltness be restored? It is no longer good for anything except to be thrown out and trodden under foot by men.

"You are the light of the world. A city set on a hill cannot be hid. Nor do men light a lamp and put it under a bushel, but on a stand, and it gives light to all in the house. Let your light so shine before men, that they may see your good works and give glory to your Father who is in heaven.

"Think not that I have come to abolish the law and the prophets; I have come not to abolish them but to fulfil them. For truly, I say to you, till heaven and earth pass away, not an iota, not a dot, will pass from the law until all is accomplished. Whoever then relaxes one of the least of these commandments and teaches men so, shall be called least in the kingdom of heaven; but he who does them and teaches them shall be called great in the kingdom of heaven. For I tell you, unless your righteousness exceeds that of the scribes and Pharisees, you will never enter the kingdom of heaven.

"You have heard that it was said to the men of old, 'You shall not kill; and whoever kills shall be liable to judgment.' But I say to you that every one who is angry with his brother shall be liable to judgment; whoever insults his brother shall be liable to the council, and whoever says, 'You fool!' shall be liable to the hell of fire. So if you are offering your gift at the altar, and there remember that your brother has something against you, leave your gift there before the altar and go; first be reconciled to your brother, and then come and offer your gift. Make friends quickly with your accuser, while you are going with him to court, lest your accuser hand you over to the judge, and the judge to the guard, and you be put in prison; truly, I say to you, you will never get out till you have paid the last penny.

"You have heard that it was said, 'You shall not commit adultery.' But I say to you that every one who looks at a woman lustfully has already committed adultery with her in his heart. If your right eye causes you to sin, pluck it out and throw it away; it is better that you lose one of your members than that your whole body be thrown into hell. And if your right hand causes you to sin, cut it off and throw it away; it is better that you lose one of your members than that your whole body go into hell.

"It was also said, 'Whoever divorces his wife, let him give her a certificate of divorce.' But I say to you that every one who divorces his wife, except on the ground of unchastity, makes her an adulteress; and whoever marries a divorced woman commits adultery.

"Again you have heard that it was said to the men of old, 'You shall not swear falsely, but shall perform to the Lord what you have sworn.' But I say to you, Do not swear at all, either by heaven, for it is the throne of God, or by the earth, for it is his footstool, or by Jerusalem, for it is the city of the great King. And do not swear by your head, for you cannot make one hair white or black. Let what you say be simply 'Yes' or 'No'; anything more than this comes from evil.

"You have heard that it was said, 'An eye for an eye and a tooth for a tooth.' But I say to you, Do not resist one who is evil. But if any one strikes you on the right cheek, turn to him the other also; and if any one would sue you and take your coat, let him have your cloak as well; and if any one forces you to go one mile, go with him two miles. Give to him who begs from you, and do not refuse him who would borrow from you.

"You have heard that it was said, 'You shall love your neighbor and hate your enemy.' But I say to you, Love your enemies and pray for those who persecute you, so that you may be sons of your Father who is in heaven; for he makes his sun rise on the evil and on the good, and sends rain on the just and on the unjust. For if you love those who love you, what reward have you? Do not even the tax collectors do the same? And if you salute only your brethren, what more are you doing than others? Do not even the Gentiles do the same? You, therefore, must be perfect, as your heavenly Father is perfect.

"Beware of practicing your piety before men in order to be seen by them; for then you will have no reward from your Father who is in heaven.

"Thus, when you give alms, sound no trumpet before you, as the hypocrites do in the synagogues and in the streets, that they may be praised by men. Truly, I say to you, they have their reward. But when you give alms, do not let your left hand know what your right hand is doing, so that your alms may be in secret; and your Father who sees in secret will reward you.

"And when you pray, you must not be like the hypocrites; for they love to stand and pray in the synagogues and at the street corners, that they may be seen by men. Truly, I say to you, they have their reward. But when you pray, go into your room and shut the door and pray to your Father who is in secret; and your Father who sees in secret will reward you.

"And in praying do not heap up empty phrases as the Gentiles do; for they think that they will be heard for their many words. Do not be like them, for your Father knows what you need before you ask him. Pray then like this:

> Our Father who art in heaven,
> Hallowed be thy name.
> Thy kingdom come,
> Thy will be done,
> > On earth as it is in heaven.

Give us this day our daily bread;
And forgive us our debts,
　　As we also have forgiven our debtors;
And lead us not into temptation,
　　But deliver us from evil.

For if you forgive men their trespasses, your heavenly Father also will forgive you; but if you do not forgive men their trespasses, neither will your Father forgive your trespasses.

"And when you fast, do not look dismal, like the hypocrites, for they disfigure their faces that their fasting may be seen by men. Truly, I say to you, they have their reward. But when you fast, anoint your head and wash your face, that your fasting may not be seen by men but by your Father who is in secret; and your Father who sees in secret will reward you.

"Do not lay up for yourselves treasures on earth, where moth and rust consume and where thieves break in and steal, but lay up for yourselves treasures in heaven, where neither moth nor rust consumes and where thieves do not break in and steal. For where your treasure is, there will your heart be also.

"The eye is the lamp of the body. So, if your eye is sound, your whole body will be full of light; but if your eye is not sound, your whole body will be full of darkness. If then the light in you is darkness, how great is the darkness!

"No one can serve two masters; for either he will hate the one and love the other, or he will be devoted to the one and despise the other. You cannot serve God and mammon.

"Therefore I tell you, do not be anxious about your life, what you shall eat or what you shall drink, nor about your body, what you shall put on. Is not life more than food, and the body more than clothing? Look at the birds of the air: they neither sow nor reap nor gather into barns, and yet your heavenly Father feeds them. Are you not of more value than they? And which of you by being anxious can add one cubit to his span of life? And why are you anxious about clothing? Consider the lilies of the field, how they grow; they neither toil nor spin; yet I tell you, even Solomon in all his glory was not arrayed like one of these. But if God so clothes the grass of the field, which today is alive and tomorrow is thrown into the oven, will he not much more clothe you, O men of little faith? Therefore do not be anxious, saying, 'What shall we eat?' or 'What shall we drink?' or 'What shall we wear?' For the Gentiles seek all these things; and your heavenly Father knows that you need them all. But seek first his kingdom and his righteousness, and all these things shall be yours as well.

"Therefore do not be anxious about tomorrow, for tomorrow will be anxious for itself. Let the day's own trouble be sufficient for the day.

"Judge not, that you be not judged. For with the judgment you pronounce you will be judged, and the measure you give will be the measure you get. Why do you see the speck that is in your brother's eye, but do not notice the log that is in your own eye? Or how can you say to your brother, 'Let me take the speck out of your eye,' when there is the log in your own eye? You hypocrite, first take the log out of your own eye, and then you will see clearly to take the speck out of your brother's eye.

"Do not give dogs what is holy; and do not throw your pearls before swine, lest they trample them underfoot and turn to attack you.

"Ask, and it will be given you; seek, and you will find; knock, and it will be opened to you. For every one who asks receives, and he who seeks finds, and to him who knocks it will be opened. Or what man of you, if his son asks him for a loaf, will give him a stone? Or if he asks for a fish, will give him a serpent? If you then, who are evil, know how to give good gifts to your children, how much more will your Father who is in heaven give good things to those who ask him? So whatever you wish that men would do to you, do so to them; for this is the law and the prophets.

"Enter by the narrow gate; for the gate is wide and the way is easy, that leads to destruction, and those who enter by it are many. For the gate is narrow and the way is hard, that leads to life, and those who find it are few.

"Beware of false prophets, who come to you in sheep's clothing but inwardly are ravenous wolves. You will know them by their fruits. Are grapes gathered from thorns, or figs from thistles? So, every sound tree bears good fruit, but the bad tree bears evil fruit. A sound tree cannot bear evil fruit, nor can a bad tree bear good fruit. Every tree that does not bear good fruit is cut down and thrown into the fire. Thus you will know them by their fruits.

"Not every one who says to me, 'Lord, Lord,'

shall enter the kingdom of heaven, but he who does the will of my Father who is in heaven. On that day many will say to me, 'Lord, Lord, did we not prophesy in your name, and cast out demons in your name, and do many mighty works in your name?' And then will I declare to them, 'I never knew you; depart from me, you evildoers.'

"Every one then who hears these words of mine and does them will be like a wise man who built his house upon the rock; and the rain fell, and the floods came, and the winds blew and beat upon that house, but it did not fall, because it had been founded on the rock. And every one who hears these words of mine and does not do them will be like a foolish man who built his house upon the sand; and the rain fell, and the floods came, and the winds blew and beat against that house, and it fell; and great was the fall of it."

And when Jesus finished these sayings, the crowds were astonished at his teaching, for he taught them as one who had authority, and not as their scribes.

MATTHEW 5, 6, 7.

NOT A NEW LAW

WHAT IS OUR STAND on the Sermon on the Mount? Is it really the way to which we are called?

It was of such decisive importance to me that the church community should think deeply about this first step of the way; for the Sermon on the Mount is the first step of the way. I felt that we must again come to the first step of the way and that we must be fully united. Then, if we really grasp the Sermon on the Mount fully, if we really believe it, nothing can frighten us, neither our own self-recognition nor financial threats nor the weakness of the community, the weakness of its composition. Then we will be adequate to the situation, just as we are, in the midst of our weakness.

I

When we were beginning to go this way, the Sermon on the Mount shook us so powerfully that I simply cannot describe it. It spoke to me and encouraged me with tremendous force and depth. To me the most vital content of the Sermon on the Mount is the essence of salt, the warming blaze of light, the nature of the city community, the life-power of the tree.

These highlights of the Sermon on the Mount make it very clear that this is not a new law, that the dedication demanded here is not in the form of a new moral assignment. Instead, it is *forgiveness*. Here is Christ, the essence of salt's strength, the light and warmth of the Holy Spirit. Here is the inward light, the clarity of the inner eye, the life-strength of the tree that bears good fruit. Here is the character of the city community as a light for the whole world. This is how we must grasp it: it is not a high-tension moralism, not a moralistic demand; instead, it is the revelation of God's real power in human life. If we in our human life take our surrender to God seriously; if God enters as the strength of light, the strength of the tree, the elemental energy which alone makes new life possible —

only then shall we live the new life. That is what is decisive.

If we were to remain Tolstoyans, interpreting the Sermon on the Mount as five new commandments, we would end in a complete fiasco. No, the clarity of the law is made still sharper here — Jesus says so. The demands are not watered down. Jesus shows that the demands are not weakened by His entry into world history; instead they are infinitely sharpened.

Of course, these are only five examples — five hundred or five thousand examples could just as easily be given — five examples of the powerful effect of this light-essence, of the life energy of this mighty fruit-bearing tree. They reveal how God works in Christ. The fulfilment of the law means that this righteousness, this justice is better than that of all the scholars and theologians. The righteousness given here is absolutely different; it cannot be attained at all by means of moral intentions, ideas and concepts. It is a completely different way of meeting these demands — the organic way. It is true, living life. Just as light flares up, just as salt sears, just as the flame shines and as sap pulses in the tree, so is this life from God. It is life, life, life!

I want to say that there is no point whatsoever in our being together if it does not have this primal life in the sense of the Sermon on the Mount.

TO BECOME TRUE MEN

WE WANT TO BECOME true men. We want to dedicate ourselves entirely to all men. This true humanity can best be shown in Jesus Christ and in His Sermon on the Mount. Love must be there, love to men. One most easily feels at home among children, for with them love simply rules, without any special purpose.

If again and again we can feel together what it means to become truly human, if again and again we can be united in finding the true attitude of service toward all men and toward the suffering of all men, if again and again we can find unity in what Jesus said and how He lived, if again and again we can agree that Jesus' nature became especially clear to us in the Sermon on the Mount, if we can again and again feel together that love is the only power we need and that this true love is given in the childlike spirit — then we actually need no longer ask who is good and what spirit it is that leads to such a life. Then we will always come very close to one another whenever we speak together.

When the Sermon on the Mount dawned on me, which happened several years ago just at the end of the war, so many deep and decisive things became clear to me that it is impossible to say them in a few words. Nor would there be any sense in enumerating them. It is much better to read the Sermon on the Mount. But I would like to tell something of what impressed me so deeply and influenced me so decisively at the time that even today I have to think about it day and night.

The justice or the goodness and social love that Jesus means in the Sermon on the Mount is something quite different from the moral teaching and the piety and the dogmatics of theologians and moralists. Why is it so different? Jesus says it in speaking of the tree, the salt, the light and the city. And when He speaks of the tree and the light and the city, He is speaking of God and of His Spirit. If we would rather not hear the word "God," we speak of the light; or we could also speak of the tree or the salt. What is the strength in the tree, the strength that brings forth fruit? What is the clarity in the tree that causes each tree to bring forth the fruit that belongs to it? Whence does the strength come to bring forth this fruit from the tree?

In this connection Jesus says, "Beware of the Pharisees and theologians, beware of the false moralists when their deeds do not correspond to their words. By the fruit the tree is known." And when Jesus speaks of the salt, He says to those who are of His Spirit, "You are the salt of the earth!" What is it in the salt that Jesus means? Jesus means the essence, the nature, the element, the being of a thing. Very well, you do not want to hear of God. But think of the being, the element, the nature, the essence of that which alone can save the world. It is an elixir, but certainly not an elixir of the devil. This is the salt of the earth, the only element that can transform the earth's total corruption, the earth's total ruin into the rebirth of the earth.

What is this element? It is that which Jesus means by the first words in the Sermon on the Mount, for the words about the salt follow immediately afterwards. In those beginning words men are told what they are like when they have

the Spirit of Jesus Christ; they are told how they
will be when they belong to God's kingdom,
when they belong to God's future. You should
read those words. What good does it do for me to
tell you this? It must burn in your hearts, it must
come alive, it must be born in your hearts, for the
heart is what Jesus speaks about.

Blessed are those who have heart. Blessed are
those who can love, who everywhere build up
unity. Blessed are those who stand with the poor;
blessed are those who themselves are poor as beggars. Blessed are they that know themselves as
beggars before the Spirit. Blessed are those who
are so poor that they hunger and thirst. Blessed
are those who feel this hunger and thirst for
justice, for the justice of the heart, of love, of
the establishment of peace in unity, for they are
the people who carry the pain of the world on
their hearts, who carry the suffering of the world
in their innermost being. They are the ones who
do not think about themselves, for their whole
heart is turned toward others.

Yet they are the people who are misunderstood
and persecuted by the others, for they are the
ones who love justice and do not take part in any
injustice. And because they do not take part in

any injustice, they are the salt of the earth. They do not take part in the injustice of Mammon. They have no wealth, no savings account, nothing in the bank, nothing invested in houses or land; they have nowhere to go when need comes to them. They have no capital. Do not gather riches on this earth; rather gather the fortune existing in love. Let your whole fortune be love, so that wherever you go hearts will be opened to you because you bring love. You will encounter hatred because you bring justice, and you will be persecuted and hounded to death for not taking part in injustice. But you will be received with great love in huts that stand ready for you, and you will be taken in because you bring love into them.

This is the treasure and the wealth that is your treasure and your wealth. In this way you will be free of all care. You will live very close to nature. You will live with the flowers and the birds, and you will not worry any more about your clothes or food, for you are the companions of the birds that find their food; you are the friends of the flowers that are clothed more beautifully than vain men want to clothe themselves.

All this is the new character of salt; it is light. What is light? Light gives complete brightness and clarity. But the light meant here is not a cold light. It is the glowing light of the hearth and the lamp; it is the light of the circle of torches, and it is the warm light that streams from the windows of the community houses, the brotherhood houses. It is the light of truth that exists in love; it is the light of love that rejoices only in truth and justice and purity. Thus it is not a sultry, dark, gloomy love of emotional passion that brings injustice. It is the love that illumines faith, that brings clarity to all things. Light is very much like salt, and the greatest resemblance is that salt consumes itself, just as the torch and the candle burn themselves up.

In the Sermon on the Mount, which is a proclamation of love, Jesus speaks of adultery, which can also consist in the thoughts and feelings of the heart. Adultery is the breaking of a relationship of faithfulness, a relationship of truthfulness, the breaking of a relationship of responsible love. Therefore it can take place already in thoughts, already in the heart. The effect of light and the effect of salt is to overcome such things. The same is true when men give each other their word. Men swear the most solemn oaths and vows in order to be believed. Jesus says, "Just by this you prove that one cannot believe you. Say simply yes or no. Be completely true."

People think they should love their friends, those who also show them love. But Jesus says, "The love I give you is this: Love your enemies. You will never again kill anyone or offend anyone. You will never kill souls or hurt hearts, for you will live in absolute love, and this love will become so complete that you will not go to law against anyone. And if someone wants to take your cloak, you will take off your jacket and give it as well. And if someone demands of you one hour's work, you will do two. And thus it will be in all things. Your life will have a kind of perfection, although you will not be saints at all. The perfection of your life will be this secret of your life: You will be very weak and you will make many mistakes; you will be very clumsy, for you will be poor in spirit and will hunger and thirst for justice. You will not be perfect, but love will be in you, and this is the gate and the way. Whatever you desire for yourselves, strive for the same for your fellow men. If you expect something from your fellow men, give the same to them. This is the way."

We do not need to speak about the very deepest and last things contained in the Sermon on the Mount, where Jesus speaks of the kingdom of God and of forgiveness of sin and of the holy name and of God's will and of redemption and liberation from all evil and of the gift of daily bread which comes from God. All this we may not understand. But this one thing we certainly do understand: There is nothing greater than love. There is nothing more holy than love. There is nothing more true than love, nothing more real than love. So let us hand our lives over to love and seal the bond of love.

SALT AND LIGHT

THE NATURE OF SALT is salt or it is nothing. The essence of salt is its action. By itself it has no purpose. Salt is there for the sake of the whole.

Whoever receives God's life and grasps the nature of the future in Jesus has taken on the character of salt. Jesus wants the essence of things. He wants their ultimate reality. What is important to Him is true being. So He never demands of anyone an attitude that does not correspond to his real inner situation. Christ sees in His friends men who have His Spirit, who breathe His life. The powers of the future world are at work in them. Unconditional love, the essence of true righteousness and of unstained purity, is revealed in their lives. The coming kingdom that encompasses the whole earth will belong to God. The true character of this kingdom is opposed to all rottenness and decay; it combats death and therefore all that is insipid, flabby and effeminate.

Death can be delayed by the use of salt. We all know that doctors postpone death and revive or maintain the regenerative power of an organ by injecting salt. The injustice of the world — sin itself — is the disease of the world soul, a disease that leads to death. The mission of the comrades of the kingdom is to be the salt of the earth and as such to stem its injustice, prevent its decay and hinder its death.

The world must perish in order to be born again. But as long as the salt that acts in the world remains salt it stands against the final revelation of evil, acting as the power which one day will renew the earth and all mankind. If the church were no longer to act as salt, it would no longer be the church, but would succumb to the dying in the world. It would have to be stamped out. If salt becomes tasteless, how shall it be salted? It is fit for nothing but to be trodden underfoot. By its nature salt is something entirely different from the food which it makes palatable. Therefore the salt of the earth should not expect the present age to turn into salt; but the presence of Jesus in the kingdom is a real and constant warning to the world that without salt it will die. Just as food is insipid and unpalatable without salt, so is the world without the church. And while mankind cannot attempt to act as its own salt, it can recognize by the action of salt the character of death and decay and how death must be combated. A corrective is placed before mankind as a goal to live up to.

Salt can have such power only as long as it is different from the surrounding mass, as long as it does not itself fall into decay. If it becomes insipid and tasteless, it can only be spat out. The salt of the earth is only where God is, where the better justice of the future kingdom is lived out and where the powers of that coming order bring forth organic life and growth. In other words, salt is present only where the victorious, living energy of God's love is at work. God himself is the creative Spirit who overcomes corruption, the living Spirit who wakens the dead, whose power of life never flags. He is the God of miracles, who can bring forth new birth out of corruption and degeneration, giving rise to well-being and joy instead of nausea and disgust.

God's power, that wells up from the depths of being to flood the whole of life, is superior to all endeavors by rotten morality and hypocritical social conventions. In God's words is the strength of salt. Here is the austere courage and manfulness that does not swim with the stream and is not infected with corruption. Here is simple and concise expression, unvarnished truthfulness that would be deadly to both the speaker and the one spoken to if love were lacking. Here is love that cannot kill, love that abstains from harming one's neighbor and no more wants to harm him than oneself. Here too is the resolution rather to pluck out the evil eye than have it corrupt the whole body. Here are loyalty and trustworthiness that never change character, whose word and love stand for ever. Here is freedom from everything outward and unessential, a freedom that is ready to sacrifice all possessions and any amount of time; for it is love, love to enemies and opponents as well as to friends and brothers. This better justice is freedom from earthly treasure, freedom from the cares and worries of possessions, a childlike joy in light and color, in God himself and all that He is and gives.

Only this life from God is the salt that counteracts the spirit of the world, the salt that is death's mortal enemy. But salt can be nothing other than salt. Whoever has the Spirit of Jesus acts as salt spontaneously. If anyone wanted to become salt without being salt from the root, from God, he would be a fool. Christ expressed His deepest vision of essential reality when He said, "You are the salt of the earth . . . you are the light of the world." He did not demand anything out of keeping with the strength given to men.

This salt, this life is the light that can be kindled only in fire; without fire one cannot expect or force it to become light. Dark Neptune cannot turn into a brilliant sun; neither can the cold light of the moon be transformed into midday warmth. All the same, pitch-black coal can be turned into a fire, radiating heat, and the whole household can gather round it for warmth. But the coal has to be ignited; it has to be burned and reduced to ashes in order to become warmth-giving light.

A light on a candlestick consumes itself to give light to all who are in the house. It serves the intimate unity of the household because its life consists in dying. If one wanted to spare the candle, one would prevent it from turning into light. But to cover up a precious, burning light would be sinful. Rob a burning candle of the free air in which the flame radiates, and it goes out; it ceases to be light.

Light is characteristic of the people of Jesus — a real brightness and warmth. As the old life is consumed it turns into life-giving strength. Shameful things can live only in the dark. Brightness leads to clarity and frankness, to simplicity and purity, to genuineness and truth. Where Jesus' influence makes men into real men, their life becomes genuine and pure. It shines into the darkness of the world around and unmasks all that is spurious and untrue, all that tries to hide .

But the light that Jesus kindles is never exhausted merely in making a situation clear. Cold light has no part in the kingdom of God. Intelligent recognition, mere insight, systematic clarity of thought and sharpness of differentiation — all this is not yet the light of which Jesus speaks here. It does us no good to try by reason alone to think for once in God's way, whereas previously we have thought only in our own way. What matters is to live in God's heart and from God's heart. The brightness of His being, like that of the sun, is inseparably joined to quickening warmth. His illumination is the joyous love that forms fellowship and draws men together, the love that flows out of the soul's fervor and must find expression in deeds that always build up and never destroy.

Sunlight flashes forth life and generates it on the earth, making it germinate and bear fruit everywhere. He who lives in the daylight belongs to life; he can find his way in the sunlight. Only night is dead, because it is cold and dark. And yet even in the life of the light and sun there is a dying. Because our life moves between day and night, our nature can gain the life of resurrection only by dying.

A light cannot radiate brightness and give off warmth without consuming itself. The greatest of men was the one to suffer most violently this dying in giving light. From the cross of Jesus the light of the world went forth. He rose out of the grave and sent His disciples to all peoples, to the ends of the earth. Only the one who, with the Crucified, experiences in himself the world's suffering and guilt and his own sin and his own forgiveness is able to serve the world with the light and strength of the Risen One.

The light we mean here is Christ himself. It is the judgment fire that comes over us to consume the old, rotten life, to lead us who are crucified with Him into a radiant life of resurrection. For there is only One who is the light of the world and shines on all who come into this world. He himself was all light. He was not entangled in any untruthfulness or impurity, lovelessness or greed. It is a glaring illusion to try to push the false light of our own life or thinking into the foreground, to want ourselves to shine without letting ourselves be burnt up and consumed in Christ. No human being can teach us what light is. To give oneself to the earth as the sun gives of its fulness can never be man's doing or man's work.

The sun directs our gaze away from itself to the life illumined and impregnated by it. Thus we speak of "sun" when we see the hills, woods and fields glowing "in the sun." The city on the hill gives its light for all who want to see it; but no one would notice it unless the sun shone on it. Whatever the sun shines on becomes sunny. Everything on which the sun casts light and warmth becomes organic life; and all life awakened by this light and warmth is organic union of individual living beings. Where there is life there is fellowship.

Just as a light on a candlestick gathers the household around it, so the city on the hill is the shining image of life community; it has organic unity in its economy and management, community of work, and a united faith and joy. The towers of a city on the hill can be seen from afar — signs of civic freedom, tokens of the city communality and symbols of fellowship in faith. Such a city is not built to be hidden, to have an isolated life for itself. Its open gates show to all the outgoing joy of open hearts.

With Jesus nothing is hidden in corners; He wants nothing furtive. His light is an all-inclusive life force that belongs to all. This force seeks to affect all relationships of life in the same way as the sun shines upon the just and the unjust. God does good to enemy and friend alike. God is there for everybody and everything. The task of His salt and His light, the task of a city on the hill, can only be to serve all, to be there for all.

There is not a single area of life that should remain unaffected by this salt and light. There is no responsibility in public life, including economics and politics, from which the city on the hill may remain aloof. Nowhere should the poison of decay be allowed to set in and not be counteracted by salt. No wickedness must be allowed to lurk in the dark without the light scaring away the horrors of night. The icy, deadly breath of hatred or of coldness of heart cannot take full possession of this earth so long as the warm love of Christ who sheds light everywhere is not removed from it.

The secret of salt's action and of warmth-radiating light lies in unmixed austerity and clarity. The responsibility which God's city on the hill bears for the remotest spheres of life is quite different from the responsibility which these spheres themselves bear. The city on the hill has a freedom, an essential quality of fellowship, which it cannot lose to any kingdom of this world, any government, any church, any political party or any other organization of this age. It serves the whole of life without letting itself be enslaved or unmanned. It combats all suffering and injustice without succumbing to the suffering and without becoming unjust itself. The city on the hill must remain salt and light. For in it lies hidden the seed of the future age.

HAPPINESS

JESUS' concern was to show His friends and all those who listened to Him the character of the world order to come and of its people. At that time — as today — everyone waited for the new order in man's innermost being and at the same time in the political and economic conditions of nations. People longed for a new kingdom of that justice of which the prophets had spoken. They knew from the prophets and felt with the certainty of the religious conscience that this justice of the prophetic state of the future had to be a social justice. They knew that this social justice must be set up so close to love and grace that it is identical with love. In God's heart, justice and grace dwell so close to one another that the movement of heart they signify is one and the same.

23

Then Jesus came, and He disclosed this justice to men, both in the depths of its nature and in its practical consequences. He showed them that the justice of the future state must be of an order completely different from that moralistic justice of the pious and holy who until then had felt they were the ones who represented justice. Through His own nature and by the clear words He spoke, He revealed that the justice God does is a living, growing power that develops organically within us, a life process that takes place in accordance with sacred laws of life.

Because of this, Jesus could not stand before men to give them commands about the right way to conduct themselves. He came to them in a very different way. In spirit and in truth He discerned the nature of those who had God's righteousness. He presented their character to men's eyes in this way: Full of bliss, happy are they who have this character, for they see God; to them belongs the kingdom of the future; they shall inherit the earth; they shall be comforted and satisfied; as sons of God they shall obtain mercy.

Because Jesus himself radiated in His nature

the organic unity of all the characteristic traits of this spirit of the future, it was impossible for anyone to try to tear any one sentence of His out of its context and set it up by itself as a law. If anyone places pacifistic action or purity of heart or any other moral or political demand by itself and uses this to claim and set up the new, he is on the wrong track. Certainly it is not possible to take part in God's kingdom without purity of heart, without vigorous work for peace; but unless the good tree is planted, the good fruit cannot be harvested. Unless the change extends to all areas, it is a lost cause to try to emulate Christ in one sphere only.

The Beatitudes cannot be dismembered. They portray the heart of the comrade of the Kingdom, and his veins cannot be cut apart. Because of this they begin and end with the same promise of possessing the kingdom of heaven. Because of this each one begins with the same attribute of inner happiness.

The disposition expressed in the Beatitudes is poverty and neediness, longing, hunger and thirst; at the same time it is generous wealth, outpouring love and kindness, energy and action for peace, an overcoming of all resistance. Here the basic motive of the heart is the pureness, cleanness and singleheartedness in which one sees God. These are people of vision, people of inner vision, who see the essential. They bear the world's suffering. They know that they in themselves are poor as beggars in the face of the Spirit. They find no righteousness within themselves. But they perceive righteousness and they see Spirit; and therefore they hunger and thirst and are full of longing. This is not the happiness of satiety; it is not the pleasure of gratifying desire. Here is disclosed that deeper happiness which is given to eyes that are opened and the open heart. Openness for God and His riches and all that He constantly gives can be found only where people again and again feel poor and empty, thirsty and hungry.

Richness in God and poverty in oneself, becoming one with God and insatiable hunger for Him, undivided resolve of the heart and weakness of the soul, the justice of God's love and the suffering of injustice — these always belong together. This paradox is the essence of true religious experience. Wherever there is religious satiety and moral self-satisfaction, wherever the self-righteousness of political achievements or other good works is to be found, wherever anyone feels rich or victorious, the happiness of the comrades of the Kingdom has no place. But where Jesus has become the guide on the simple way of discipleship, there those people can be found who know the happiness of God's kingdom and who believe in the justice of God's future. Their hearts are fixed undividedly on the Spirit and His prophetic justice of complete love, and they feel the injury of injustice in themselves and around them. They feel the poverty of spirit in their own lives and in all mankind. But they envision the justice of God's kingdom and they feel comforted by the certainty that love shall conquer the earth.

Thus they are both poor and rich at the same time. For they are people of faith, people who have nothing in themselves and possess everything in God; who in spite of failures venture over and over again to make the invisible real and who take nothing away from the absolute nature of God's love. Just as they themselves receive mercy, they pour mercy out upon all who are in need; they know they are on the side of poverty and suffering, on the side of all those who suffer injury, and they are ready to be per-

secuted with them for the sake of justice. They
know that they cannot traverse the world without struggle. They know that their opponents'
slander must fall on them like a hailstorm. But
they rejoice in this struggle and they remain the
peacemakers who overcome opposition everywhere and who conquer enmity through love.
The people of the Beatitudes are the people of
love; they live from God's heart and are at
home in His heart. They are the ones whom the
law of the Spirit of life has set free from the law
of sin and death; they are the ones who cannot
be separated by any power from the love of God
which is in Christ Jesus.

The most remarkable thing about the mystery
of these people, however, is that everywhere
they perceive the same seed of God and see the
same light gleaming and feel the same warm
rays. Wherever human beings break down under
the world's suffering, wherever hearts feel their
own poverty and long for the Spirit, wherever
the ardent revolutionary desire for social justice
arises, wherever the passionate protest against
war and bloodshed rings out, wherever people
are persecuted because of their pacifism or their
feeling for social justice, wherever purity of

heart and genuine compassion are to be found—
there they hear His footsteps in history, there
they see the approach of His kingdom, there
they anticipate the blissfulness to come.

There is no other way to prepare inwardly for
the coming Kingdom than the one way Jesus
shows us here. If we want to enter on this way,
we can do nothing else but to admit, without
qualification and without excuse, our poverty
of spirit. Everything else disappears and becomes utter nothingness for us when we feel that
our hunger and thirst for the one justice of
complete love is the essential thing that opens
our hearts for what God alone can give.

THE NATURE OF THE NEW JUSTICE

THE SERMON ON THE MOUNT reveals Jesus' heart to us. It confronts us with His actual will. That great decision which comes to us in the Sermon on the Mount is already introduced by the outward fact that there is a meeting of a large crowd of people; that Jesus' disciples throng around Him; that He speaks to the whole crowd; that He looks at His disciples, thus addressing His words to them.

Jesus always means all people. But what He sees among people is those who are or are to become His disciples. He knows that all are poor and empty; but He brings happiness and wealth for all those very ones who because they see and feel their poverty are open to what He gives. The Sermon on the Mount cannot be a law that demands a certain moral effort, a certain exertion of energy; for it seeks a vacuum, it presupposes that emptiness, that utter poverty which has nothing to show for itself and can achieve nothing.

In Luke these things are written without qualifying words. Blessed are you poor! Happiness to you who hunger and thirst! Blessed are you who weep! Blessed are you when you are persecuted! There is no hint of a specialized religious sphere of life; instead, the characteristic mark of the comrades of the Kingdom is expressed as the simple fact that they are poor, that they hunger and thirst, that they bear suffering, that they are despised and maligned.

Luke therefore cannot leave unsaid the words directed to the opposite side. Woe to you that are rich! Woe to you that are full! Woe to you that laugh! Woe to you of whom men only speak well! This "Woe!" applies wherever anything is felt to be a possession, as the substance of life, as admirable, or even merely as something commonly recognized. For here the basic condition necessary for the Kingdom — a being empty in oneself — is lacking.

In Matthew this utter poverty is disclosed in its ultimate depths as poverty in spirit, that is, an emptying in the things of the spirit, in things of religion, in things of morals and wisdom. It is a mourning for everything in the world and it is mourning for what is in oneself. It is mourning for individuals and for the conditions of the world as a whole; for guilt both individual and collective; for material need and for the deepest need of the soul. In this connection, therefore, the necessary persecution and contempt must be shown as a persecution for the sake of justice, for the sake of that other justice free of moralism which is most hated by those who want to be righteous in a certain wealth of possessions, of correctness, of morals and religion.

The nature of this other justice is the topic of the Sermon on the Mount. This justice is blissfulness in poverty. It is the mystery of the change of heart, of that radical change proclaimed by John, the last prophet of the first Judaism. He had foretold that new order of things which all prophets had seen in their visions. He had proclaimed it as a coming onto the earth, as a coming down from heaven; as the decisive approach of God. He had proclaimed God as justice for all men and for all things; God as joy for the individual, as the

fellowship of all. Into this justice of the future—
which is nothing but God himself — Jesus
allowed himself to be immersed as in a watery
grave in which the present life on earth is
continually condemned to death.

The entire Sermon on the Mount shows us
what the characteristics of this new justice are
as a gift given by the future, as a promise given
in God himself. The God of this goodness is the
God of creation, the ultimate mystery of life,
the origin of procreation of life and of living
growth. Thus this justice cannot exist at all
where it is a matter of the goodness and
achievement of man as he is today. Among
men this justice appeared only once, in the Son
of man, in Jesus. It is present today in the Risen
One; in His Spirit it is active, working as the
power of the Creator, who is the God of
resurrection.

The Sermon on the Mount, then, shows us the
character of Jesus himself and therefore the
character of His kingdom, the essence of His
Spirit. Here there can be no self-awareness of
human goodness or nobility, no standing on
rights and no resistance by one person to
another. Here God's love is given as strength

and joy; for here, having nothing means having everything.

The knowledge of the Sermon on the Mount can be opened up only to those who know something of reverence for the Creator: who sense that also all powers of body and soul in the life of natural, organic growth are an outright gift from God and utterly dependent on Him. God's creation can never be regarded as the effort of men, as a more or less profitable field for their activity. The new creation in Christ's Spirit has nothing to do with the efforts of will by contemporary individuals or by mankind as a whole as it is today. Jesus, therefore, cannot say, "You should be light, you should be salt, you should make yourselves into a city!" Instead, He recognizes that the creation and the new creation is a being and a becoming which evolves and has its being from the Creator. You are the salt of the earth, you are the light of the world. Salt is salt, or it is less than dung; it is dirt that is fit only to be thrown away. Light burns and shines and warms. If it does not do this, it is not light. Light, like salt, does its task by consuming itself. Here we are concerned with a giving up of one's own life, which then becomes happy in its task, its giving up. The task of love, the self-effacing, blissful devotion to the task — this is the essence of Jesus and His kingdom.

Only out of such love can fellowship arise. Just as a medieval township lets the landmarks of freedom, of common faith and common work [cathedrals] be seen from afar, so too, the new life that comes over men from God carries on its activity freely in unity and work.

It is just as impossible to *make* a communal life of this kind as it would be to produce a tree in a factory. The building up of the church community, coming into being out of the spirit of community, is an action by God just as free and independent of human activity as the creation of a tree and its fruit. As the tree is, so is the fruit. Creation's law of growth and life is here placed in opposition to human doings, just as in the Letter to the Romans the law of the Spirit of life is opposed to the law of sin and death. Living creation takes the place of dead weight.

What man can never accomplish, God does. His creative Spirit is the secret of the law of life, for God is a God of all that is living, not a God of death. The resurrection of Jesus is the ultimate revelation of this law of life. The Sermon on the Mount can be grasped only where reverence for the Creator and the creation is overwhelmed by the Spirit of the resurrection; where Jesus is proven in power to be the Son of God, through this very Spirit of holy consecration whose action goes out from the resurrection. Outside of this the Sermon on the Mount remains an impossibility, a utopia, unwholesome fantasy, nonsense, self-deception or madness.

The seed died and lay in the soil; only its bursting forth, living out of death, means fruits for all. The life that spreads out from here is a gift that tries to embrace everything living, a gift of life that is the mortal enemy of death alone. In this sphere there can be no killing of life; there can be no hatred toward other men, in whom there also slumbers the same germ of divine life; there can be no insisting on any human cause, which is never life itself. Thus liberating love alone can be the fulfilment of this life; for only the love that lifts us out of the human sphere, love such as *God* has, affirms and bestows all that is living. Only God has this perfect life that sends His sun to all — on sinners and moralists, on the just and the unjust, on seekers of God and blasphemers of God. This is what makes His justice so thoroughly different from that of all the moralists and theologians, which always and everywhere finds it necessary to emphasize the boundaries and differences, the solid walls and closed doors.

God's heart is mercy, that is, love to all. It wants justice in external things, just as it wants mercy on the soul, because it is the "soul of all mercy." Thus Luke closes his words about the attitude of the comrades of the Kingdom with the simplest practical watchword. Love! Be merciful from your hearts! Hold on to nothing for yourselves. Do not judge. Do not seek faults in others. Give to all. Give to your enemies.

This attitude means reconciling; it means not resisting; it means giving up all rights. It demands an ever increasing expenditure of time and strength and life, when the first step of giving oneself has provoked nothing but enmity or antipathy. The deepest reason for this is the positive, creative, constructive drive in this love, which through opposition has to be stimulated and awakened to more energetic effort. Wherever antagonism appears, wherever any hostility turns up, the impulse to dedication is strengthened.

Neighbors and enemies — these two are the only beings with whom there can be a living relationship. Nowhere does any other love exist but the love to neighbors and the love to enemies. Jesus' witness turns to both with equal power. The love to one's neighbor which Jesus equates with love to God is for Him inseparably bound up with unconditional love to one's enemy.

This love, arising from God, overflows toward both sides; it is this love which is proclaimed in the Sermon on the Mount. Toward neighbors as toward enemies, it must prove itself as faithfulness and truthfulness. In the symbol of marriage, which is the symbol of the unity of two in creative power, in the plain truthfulness of the simple yes and no, this love is shown to be constantly the same faithfulness and truth, in the joy as much as in the struggle of human relations.

Anyone who dares to live by this spirit stands ever anew before the infinite, the boundless. Often he trembles as before a bottomless abyss;

for on this way, things as they are do not afford
a foothold anywhere. And yet his lungs fill up
over and over again with endless purity and
strength, for the air which this spirit wafts to
him is eternal breath of God; it is God himself
as Spirit. But again, it threatens to burst us
apart. For our lungs cannot comprehend the
infinite. Here we are always condemned and
pardoned, always poverty-stricken and exces-
sively rich, always killed and awakened at the
same time.

Here the laws of antipathy, sympathy and
elective affinity yield; here economic problems
do not call a halt. Here we no longer find some
people more valuable and others more unfit.
Here everything that is loud and conspicuous
comes to a stop; germinating life is hidden life.
Creation lives and works in quietness. Like the
harmony, soundless to us, of the cherubim and
the galaxies in their eternal worship of God, so
too the prayer of men is what is most hidden
and chaste in the life that comes from God. The
Father seeks life in what is hidden. The remote
mountain, the untenanted steppe and the closed
chamber are the places of final decision. Because of this, these most secluded hours are

brief and clear by nature, for the mass of words
is noise and hubbub. Their simple content can
after all be only the one thing — the kingdom of
God on earth, His will being done among men;
the transformation, coming from God, of all
relationships in life; daily bread for all;
forgiveness and protection.

The Sermon on the Mount stands in the
midst of that prophetic context to which Jesus
joined His life with the words of the Baptist:
Change yourselves fundamentally; the kingdom
of God has come near. What is meant is protection from the hour of temptation which points
to that shattering, catastrophic revolution which
is to come over the whole earth. Out of the
urgency of this final decision a new attitude
in life must be born: voluntary poverty, as
the matter-of-course expression of trust and
devotion.

Here it makes no difference what kind of
riches we have. For anything and everything
the same is true. Gather no riches for yourselves!
Know only the one single treasure, the treasure
in heaven. There can be only one object for
your longing. Either your longing, your heart,
is set on things, or else your inward eye is

directed toward that which is entirely different. Here any dividedness of heart means darkening and judgment. You can never serve God and money at the same time. Nothing but the heart is decisive here. Consequently, to worry about material things and one's living arises from the same anti-divine spirit of Mammon as the accumulating of wealth.

Life that is given by God liberates from both worry and possession. Just as the birds and flowers in creation are cared for, so in the new creation there is abundance of food and clothing wherever trust in God acknowledges His kingdom as the first and the last thing, as that which alone matters. Everything else follows as a matter of course. Anyone whose heart is turned toward the future kingdom cannot be controlled by these things any more.

A simple rule of life arises here naturally which can help us on this way. Never burden yourselves with a view reaching across long periods of time; always live for one day at a time. If you can do this, you will live like children, like birds and flowers. For them each day is a lifetime. For every day unfolds new joy and new hope. Every day may have brought

you new shadows and new nightfall. Every day
you may have broken down again in guilt
and failure. Every day may have shown us a
thousandfold our helplessness when faced with
the life shown in the Sermon on the Mount.
Yet — the new day is new sun, new air, new
grace.

So trust grows, trust in God and trust in
those in whom God works. Jesus encourages all
who obey Him to pray and to believe ever anew.
He promises that when we ask, it shall be given.
We can enter as into an open gate that leads
into a big garden. God's garden has an open
door. It is narrow, but it is there for all. Whoever knocks and enters will have the door
opened for him.

Luke says clearly what the object of this
asking and believing and waiting and daring
is. It is the Spirit! If you evil men give your
children good food, truly you can rely on God
to give you what you need — the Holy Spirit.
Everything that is contained in the Sermon on
the Mount is done by this Spirit. It is the lamb's
nature as opposed to that of the wolf. Only
out of its matterless matter does God's new
creation arise, that rebirth that turns wolves

into lambs, that transforms the horrible predacious realm made by men into God's kingdom of peace.

All the more, however, it is necessary to realize that nobody should be deceived by signs and gestures, by busyness and bustle. Jesus wants all to be on their guard against being deceived by soft, lamb-like words, while the unbroken wolf nature lies in ambush. Its characteristic mark is the grasping, rapacious will. It is a matter here of distinguishing the spirits, of not giving what is holy to dogs and swine — and yet not judging. The judge speaks out a final verdict, which removes trust. He stands in a different place from the condemned man. No man has the right to do this; for only God judges in such a way that He saves. We men all sit on the same bench, we are all in the same boat.

The Sermon on the Mount judges us all, for it discloses our evil fruits, by which the evil tree must be recognized. No plan, however well intentioned, no formulation of truth, however correct, can belie this fact: the fruit of the deed, the doing of God's justice, the new love for all that flows from the heart, is what marks the newness of life that is meant by the Sermon on the Mount. Where these words of Jesus become life and action, there is the firm building of God which cannot be overthrown even in the final catastrophe. Where they do not become action, the only thing that can be expected is what human deeds truly are — a heap of rubble.

"BUT I SAY TO YOU..."

UNTIL JESUS APPEARED, the greatest goodness man could offer his God was moral endeavor. It was ethical striving, strenuous effort toward an ideal goal, an effort scrupulously to obey commands and prohibitions, laboriously to repress and stifle contrary inclinations. Sometimes man even made frenzied, ecstatic attempts to deny and mortify himself and life as such. Men felt they had to gather together all their human forces for a laborious ascent or a frantic charge up a mountain where the light would not be obscured or the air polluted.

Jesus brings a justice that is better than that offered by any of these human strivings, because His justice is different in every sense from all that the law and the prophets were able to say. Certainly law and prophets contain a revelation of God's being and God's will; and Jesus does not wish in any way to undo or obscure the incorruptible clarity of this revelation. If anyone were to presume to act in opposition to God's clear and definite will in a way that confuses and breaks down these moral commands and prohibitions, he would be sinning against that holy thing which God has laid in men's consciences. If men were to lose this holy thing, they would no longer have any refuge or security whenever the sinister powers of lying and untruth, of hate and greed, hound them from one situation to another until finally, having no support, they would fall prey to death.

The fact is that not one letter of these ethical commands and moral prohibitions will be canceled for men until the essential thing hidden behind these laws has been revealed and represented, has taken on flesh and life. These commands and prohibitions express as law the holy "thou shalt" of our inner calling, the holy "must" of our inner destiny; they express that which alone is the absolute that lives in the human soul. Those who belong to the growing number who try today to declare one after the other of these laws null and void and to reject them will be poorly prepared for God's kingdom.

Until the decisive hour when God's Word became flesh and reality in Jesus, God chose an almost petrified form, a demanding and forbidding, to express the essence of His holiness. For there was no being in whom God's holiness could be embodied in living form in equally unbroken clarity. The purity of God's will had to fall back on the letter of the law tablets, because there was no living heart to give it a living and unfeigned expression.

Wherever the plain truthfulness and purity of Jesus' heart, the generous love of His Spirit that knows no greed, has not yet taken root, the law must take over if everything is not to be destroyed. The state with its violence and the law with its statute books are a necessary safety valve for the witches' brew of a chaotic, inorganic mass of people. Just as the steam would burst the boiler and disperse to nothing, so the opposing and scattering elements would necessarily burst, fragment, and ruin everything if the iron boiler of governmental force with the safety valves of its laws were not there.

A completely different situation is given as

soon as people are gripped by God's love. They grow toward one another and become organs of a mysterious unity, of a mystical body which, ruled by a spirit of unity, is one heart and one soul. Here the necessity for force and coercion, for law and moral striving is done away with, because the true Spirit, which the law expressed imperfectly, has come to rule. The better and wholly other righteousness which Jesus brought is goodness of heart, organic strength from God, which, working through the soul, embraces all of human existence. It is the justice of mankind's future; it no longer needs to take into account the mutual restraints and injuries that are part of our present legal relationships.

This new justice is unconquerable, because it is God's goodness itself. It can be neither weakened nor changed, for it is the manifestation of a life energy that seeks to unfold everywhere and to be applied to every area of life. This justice is goodness itself, because God is good. His goodness is love; His justice reveals all the powers of His love. Any attempt to be as good as this on the basis of legal regulations, principles or traditions is doomed to failure from the outset. For that kind of justice could never be bursting, overflowing life. It could never produce anything more than laborious effort, a forcing oneself to fit into armor, into patterns that do not spring from life itself.

The scribes and the Pharisees had a firm conviction, a moral direction and an iron will. They were better than their reputation; they were morally upright, devout figures who commanded respect, men who felt deeply their responsibility for their people, for morals and religion. But what they lacked was the free Spirit that blows from God. What they did not have was the gift of life from God, the life that must grow and bear fruit just because it is there. What they lacked was being filled with Holy Spirit. What they lacked was God himself.

God cannot be imitated. His power can be replaced by nothing. His nature cannot be duplicated. We cannot compel ourselves to love. The first works of the first love cannot be artificially manufactured. No intelligent reflection, no moral resolution or effort of will can produce the warmth of heart that is of God. Morals and the law are replaced by the warm life of God's love. Jesus overcame morals and moralism by something better, by God's own life, which can only be vaguely suggested by laws. Where He lives, active love has taken the place of dead moralism.

Jesus brings a wholly different righteousness. He brings God's goodness because He brings God himself, who encompasses everything and tolerates nothing isolated; the living God, who wants nothing but life; the God of riches, whose being consists in giving; the God of radiating light and flooding warmth. Only those who lose themselves in God have the new justice. Only where God himself lives and works does this justice of the warmly pulsing heart take the place of the stony tablets of the law.

AWAY FROM COMPROMISE
AND SHADOW

IT IS NOT BY CHANCE that in our periodical, *Wegwarte,* a discussion has arisen about compromise and about the shadow with which one must come to terms because it is there everywhere and at all times. Dormant behind this lies the fundamental life problem, the question about evil and about death, which concerns all serious-minded people again and again. Evil and death are so oppressively heavy that good and life constantly threaten to fall victim to them. In all the circles of the larger Movement [The Christian Youth Movement] with which *Wegwarte* readers are in any kind of contact, that slackening of purpose, that avoidance of the either-or, as represented among us by Heinrich Euler and his friends, has spread in a frightening way.

The large Movement itself had been awakened by the coming light and had turned away from compromise with today's darkness. It was clear to its members that with evil there can be no compromise. The word compromise has its origin in the language of law. It means a mutual settlement between contending parties. Well and good — it belongs where there is legal conflict. It is a settlement between opposing parties who are both fighting for, say, the same property; it is compromise on which the court of arbitration must insist.

Our problem, however, is the question whether one can set a better justice, that of the all-bestowing heart of Jesus' Sermon on the Mount, in the place of this highest justice from the point of view of law. This means that, when faced with the threat of a legal battle, the one who wants to go the way of life and of love will give everything up, that is, allow his opponent to take everything away from him, rather than compromise. Here we are met, not by hard demands on our ever futile efforts, but by assurances of the deepest powers, opportunities for overflowing joy and love.

The news of the new life is this: bringing

joy excludes murder; love hates no man; truth strikes no compromise with lying; the heart can remain pure only by making no concessions; the Father of Jesus who gives everything comes to no mutual settlement with Mammon, least of all in a heart that belongs to Him. In short, joy in love, love for all, tolerates no compromise with death, no concession to loveless indifference or murderous injustice and brutality, because the way of love reaches out to all men, touches all things, overturns all relationships. This is the news of the new life, the message of the Kingdom, the character of Jesus' words. Here is His heart.

Every movement that comes from God, from His life, is concerned with this way. And whenever such a living movement of hearts dies, this way is deserted. The process of dying reaches the final stage of death when wrestling with death is given up, when the struggle for life is deserted and men surrender unresisting to the shadow of death. Here too it is altogether a matter of that natural dying which threatens every movement; it is a desertion to Philistinism and mediocrity; it is a stepping out from that struggle to which Jesus has called us.

The fact that people try to live simultaneously on the basis of the law and on the basis of grace; that a life of nonviolence in this age is called fiction, humbug and vapor, whereas Jesus, after all, went this way; that people fight against an uncompromising stand and think that by doing so they oppose both legalism and fanaticism; that they want to say an unqualified yes to the sphere of earthly life; that they are actually infatuated with the shadow of bad and evil and take pains to show that one can never get rid of this shadow and that basically it makes no difference at all whether there is more compromise or less compromise — all this shows how far off the way they have come.

Max Dressler shows us the chief point in the new life, that only the experience of love in the full forgiveness of sin can bring healing and that in this atmosphere the legalistic "thou shalt" and "thou shalt not" cease to be. This cannot be emphasized strongly enough. But is it not disconcerting if the only possible consequence for practical life from the experience of this love is not drawn here: He who is forgiven much loves much. How can we love God, whom we do not see, if we do not love the brother, whom we see?

Yes, there is only one way, the way of love, the love that comes from forgiveness and has its essence in forgiveness. And this way is absolute discipleship of Jesus, making no compromise with all that is loveless in these times. Of course, this does not mean that one who is gripped by love never makes compromises; rather, it means that the love which has gripped him can make no compromises. If he nevertheless does what is evil, this comes from the badness and weakness of his character. But whenever love again takes hold of him and fills him with its glowing warmth, he will once more set his eyes on the highest goal and begin anew to live the word of Jesus, which means the power of perfect love and nothing else.

This fact is uncompromisingly expressed in the First Letter of John. Whoever claims he is without sin is a liar. We are told this so that we may not sin. But if we do sin, we have an Advocate who expiates the sin of the whole world. Whoever abides in Him does not sin. If anyone sins, then in this sin he has not seen and known Him. "We know that we are of God, and the whole world is in the power of evil."

Whoever defends sin shows by this attitude

that he has gone astray from recognizing Jesus, from seeing Jesus; in speaking this way he neither saw nor recognized Him.

It makes a great deal of difference whether the evil that we do lies before us because we want to do it, or whether it lies behind us, so that we forget it and leave it. For Paul it was essential to leave everything behind and to race full tilt toward the goal with his eyes set on nothing but the goal itself. There is no doubt that it was always clear to him, and he testified to it very deeply, that this did not mean that he had no guilt. But the forgiveness that Christ brings means liberation from wrong and evil. Because of this Paul was a fighter who fought in his full armor against all evil and against death itself.

It is very significant that uncompromising love has nothing to do with softness or flabbiness, nothing to do with a nonfighting attitude. On the contrary, the resolute will for peace has to carry on a fight of the spirits against all spiritual powers that are opposed to peace and love. In this fight it is out of the question to injure or kill one's fellow men for the very reason that no human judgment can judge them as ultimately evil, as finally rejected, as forfeited to death. All the more sharply must this fight of the spirits be waged against everything in each person himself and in his fellow men that is recognized to be inimical to life, injurious to life, hostile to fellowship, directed against God.

The man who is permeated with life and gripped by love is a fighter to the point of shedding his blood. He is never hard toward his fellow men, though it may be felt as hardness when in the passion of glowing love he struggles in volcanic exuberance against all the bad and evil that he meets within himself and in his fellow men and in the public state of affairs. His fight is a completely private matter which can be led to personal decision only in the deepest mutual relationship between him and God alone; but it is also at the same time a very public matter in which in all public questions he must take a determined stand in opposition to all human conditions as they are.

The attitude of such a fighter for love will be erroneously regarded as moralistic or even legalistic. His ethic, that is, his conduct toward his fellow men and to all mankind's works and institutions, is clearly defined in its content;

defined, that is, by the goal of God's kingdom, defined by the character of the Son of man and His comrades of the Kingdom, defined by the truth of love, by the will of God's heart. This will is the life of complete love, the attitude of the future world; it is the perfection of God in which we must live, because there is no other life.

This brings us to the age-old topic of perfection and sinlessness. It is certain that in the here and now, as *we* are, there is no sinless state. But the way people everywhere speak nowadays about the necessity of evil and about men's common bondage in guilt unquestionably leads to something like consent to involvement in guilt. People ironically dismiss the world peace to which the prophets witness, the elimination of government proclaimed in John's Revelation, the overcoming of the present social order which comes with brotherhood in church community; they dismiss the communal life which should be — and has been again and again — the self-evident expression of true love. The irony with which people try to dismiss all these things shows quite clearly that in all these critical areas they no longer want to take a stand against evil. They avoid the great either-or that Jesus has shown us: God or Mammon.

By doing this, people turn away from the clarity with which Jesus challenged us to say clearly yes or no, never something between the two, never no when it should be yes or yes when it should be no. Today people turn away from the way of Jesus in the vanity of weak acceptance of man's paradoxical situation in relation to God; all they can say is yes and no or no and yes at the same time to everything all the time and everywhere. Against this we must take up the fight.

One of the present leaders in the dying Movement, who dissolves into speculative paradoxes the decisiveness with which the formerly flaming Youth Movement was charged by God, once called to one of us in a youth meeting, "Surely you don't want to wage a general campaign against all evil?" Yes, this is exactly what it is all about. It was for this that Jesus came to the world; He called us and sent us out so that we might take up and carry on this campaign against all evil in all fields and in all things. He came to destroy the works of the devil. God is light and in Him there is no darkness.

AGAINST BLOODSHED AND VIOLENCE

AGAIN AND AGAIN, in the life of the nation, between the nations and in the class struggle for existence, we experience violent outbursts of accumulated tensions and conflicts. These outbursts reveal the existing state of mutual exploitation and oppression, and, last but not least, the savage instincts of chaotic, covetous passion. This volcanic eruption of bloodthirsty, inordinate passions and of merciless countermeasures has intensified and spread to such an extent from various quarters, that it is necessary to say a clear word here.

Others may see their task in the upholding of law and order by murderous means; others may believe they are called to fight for the proletariat, for a future of justice and peace with blood-stained fists; others may regard their own race as a holy shrine and declare war on another race. Our life is filled with a content which has deeper roots. A life task has been entrusted to us which looks further ahead. The mystery of life has been revealed to us. It has dawned upon us, because Christ means everything to us. We feel united with the whole church of Christ, in which no group or individual can live in isolation from the rest. Both the one and the other are members and organs of the one living body, the Spirit, head and heart of which is the coming Christ. Hence the testimony of our life is nothing but the essence of His own life. He discloses the mystery of life to us when He points to the birds in the air at springtime, to the flowers in the meadow, when He expects good fruits only from the healthy tree, when He reveals the heart of the Father to us, who sends His rain and His sunshine on both the good and the bad.

Life is growth and development. Life is the unfolding of love. Killing does not belong to life. It belongs to death. Violence and coercion do not belong to growth but to the stifling of life. The witness has been entrusted to us to live for only that which serves life and builds

life. It makes no difference whether the growth
of this life appears to be evolutionary or revolutionary. It is both at the same time, development
and upheaval, because life means to cast off
that which wants to die. Life means to give and
bestow what awakens life. Yet no evolution, no
upheaval is able to eradicate the deepest root of
all world suffering: universal guilt, the lethal
poison of evil, of hate, covetous lust, depravity
and killing.

The new birth is brought about by organic
life. It springs from the same God who is at
work in all that is living. Yet for a new beginning it always brings with it a tearing away, a
toppling over of the old, a painful liberation.
Every individual and the whole of mankind is
in need of this new birth.

We believe in this new birth of a life of light
from God. We believe in the future of love and
in the constructive fellowship of men. We believe in the peace of God's kingdom, that He
will come to this earth. This faith is not a
playing with a future shape of things which
exists only in our imagination now. No. The
same God who will bring this future gives us
His heart and His spirit today. His name is the

I Am Who I Am. His nature is the same now as it will reveal itself in the future. He revealed His heart in Jesus. He gives us His Spirit in Christ's presence among us. In His church, the embodiment of Christ's life, He lives the life of Jesus once again. This church is the hidden living seed of the future Kingdom. The character of peace and the love-spirit of the future have been entrusted to her. Therefore she practices justice and peace and joy in this world, also in the present age.

We speak up in protest against bloodshed and violence from the reality of this life-witness, no matter from which side these powers of death may come. Our witness and our will for peace, for love at any cost, also at the cost of our own lives, has never been more necessary than it is today. Those are in error, who reproach us that at a time when this question is not at all urgent, we are speaking of defencelessness, non-violence, conscientious objection, of discipleship of Jesus in the power of radiating love, which makes all violence impossible and excludes us from inflicting any kind of injury on others. This question is more urgent today than it ever was, and it will become evident, that loyal perseverance in an attitude of absolute love requires ultimate courage, manly courage unto death.

Jesus knew that He would never be able to conquer the earth spirit by greater violence, but only by greater love. This is why He overcame the temptation to somehow seize power over the kingdoms of this earth. He proclaimed the rulership of God, which is of the present and of the future at the same time. God's will was present in His life, in His deeds, His words and in His suffering. This is why in His Sermon on the Mount, He speaks of men who are strong by love, of the peacemakers, of the men of the heart, who will inherit the land and possess the earth, to whom the kingdom of God belongs. He took up the ancient proclamation of peace, the ancient message of justice, which belongs to the future kingdom of God. He deepened the crucial word of life: "Thou shalt not kill," which rules out murder in every instance, because it is the original, the very first sacrilege against life. He shows men that any cruel handling, any brutal violation of the inner life of men, falls under the same word: it injures body and soul, yes God, just as much as the killing of the body.

It is a matter of deepest regret, therefore, that serious-minded Christians today do not have this simple and clear witness of Jesus and primitive Christianity, which living biblical churches and movements in other centuries represented and proclaimed so strongly. Living Christians who took a determined attitude in life, felt that war and the military profession are irreconcilable with the calling of Christianity. There certainly must be police. forces today. The service of such forces is more ethical than the competition of two business concerns in which only one of them is able to survive. But what we are concerned with here is a completely different question, it is the question of the mission and testimony of Christ, the question of the church and the task she has been commissioned to do.

We do not deny radical evil and sin, we do not deny the end of the world. But we do not believe in evil; we believe in God and His end of the world, we believe in the rebirth of the earth and of mankind. This faith is not evolutionism, a belief in the inevitable ascent to ever greater, more visible perfection. On the contrary, this faith believes in the growth of

the divine seed in the consciences of men, in the
Christ-spirit, in the rebirth of the individual, in
the fellowship of the church. But it also believes
in the upheaval of world catastrophe, of world
judgement in war, revolution and other horrors
of the end, it believes in the collapse of this
depraved and degenerate world of compulsion
and coercion.

This faith expects everything from God and
from God alone. It is certain, however, that
God's seed and God's light is at work in all men,
and that He reveals His heart and His future
kingdom in the church of Christ. It is certainly
true that the tension between the anti-Christian
power and the Christ-life is present everywhere
today, also in the midst of the Christian church.
It will become stronger the more radically
we hold on to faith in absolute love and in that
which is coming in the future. Faith does not
fear the collision between the anti-Christian and
the Christ-worked spiritual forces; rather does
faith expect and long for this conflict because
the end must come at last, and after it the
completely new world.

It is an error to think that Jesus only wanted
to feed the hungry soul. Jesus concerned Himself

just as much with the body of the individual as with his soul. Jesus took over the message of the future world order of peace and justice from John the Baptist and the prophets of the Old Testament just as surely and determinedly as he took over the proclamation of the rebirth of the individual.

Because we know there are many today who cannot respond to the old biblical language any more, or are not yet able to do so, we tell the same message in a new way, as often as this is given to us. This is why we close this confession with the words of Hermann Hesse about the word of life, "Thou shalt not kill," published in his magazine *Vivos Voco* in March 1919:

"We are not yet men; we are still on our way to humanity. Every pupil of Lao-tse, every disciple of Jesus, every follower of Francis of Assisi was further ahead, much further ahead, than the laws and reasonings of present-day civilization. Yet the sentence, 'Thou shalt not kill' has been honored faithfully and obeyed by thousands of people for thousands of years. There has always been a minority of well-meaning people who had faith in the future, who obeyed laws which are not listed in any worldly code. As soldiers they showed compassion and respected their enemies, even during the last, horrible war, or refused steadfastly to kill and hate when ordered to do so, suffering imprisonment and torture for this.

"To appreciate these people and what they did, to overcome the doubt, that animals will be human one day, we must live in faith. We must consider thoughts to be just as valuable as bullets or coins. The so-called 'practical' man is always wrong. The future, the idea, faith, is always right.

"And we who believe in the future will raise the ancient demand again and again, 'Thou shalt not kill.' It is the basic demand of all progress, of all true humanity which is to come.

"We kill at every step, not only in wars, riots, and executions. We kill when we close our eyes to poverty, suffering, and shame. For the consistent socialist all property is theft. In the same way all disrespect for life, all hardheartedness, all indifference, all contempt is nothing else than killing in the eyes of the consistent believer of our kind. It is possible to kill not only what is in the present, but also that which is in the future. With just a little witty scepticism we can kill a good deal of the future in a young person. Life is waiting everywhere, the future is flowering everywhere, but we only see a small part of it and step on much of it with our feet. We kill with every step.

"This is why, above all, every one of us has a personal task to do. This task is not to help on the whole of mankind a little; it is not the improvement of some institution, not the abolition of a particular kind of killing. All this is good and necessary, too. But the most important task for you and me, my fellow human being, is this: to take a step forward, in our own, singular personal life, from animal to man."

THE BETTER RIGHTEOUSNESS

IN THE SERMON ON THE MOUNT, Jesus portrays the character of His kingdom. Here the inner nature of the comrades of the kingdom finds its definitive form. Here is the new ethic of a better justice, founded on a unique experience of God.

The old morality, described by Jesus as the "righteousness of the scribes and Pharisees," is an outward righteousness brought about by the legalism and coercion of society, church and state. The better righteousness, in contrast, shows that its nature is inner freedom. Independent of outward circumstances, this better righteousness allows nothing and no one to impose upon it conditions which direct its life from outside. For this reason it is in opposition to mammonistic servility and builds alone upon God and fellowship with Him.

The character of the comrades of the kingdom differs so sharply from that of all other men that it can be compared only with the nature of the Father in heaven. "You, therefore, must be perfect, as your heavenly Father is perfect."

God is the wellspring of life; He is life-giving Spirit, overflowing love. It is only by new birth out of this Spirit of the Father that we become His children and gain His character. Both the Sermon on the Mount in the Gospel of Matthew and the talk with Nicodemus in the Gospel of John proclaim and lead us into the mystery of community with God, the unity of the soul with God himself.

The new life as Jesus presents it in the Sermon on the Mount can be attained only through that fundamental experience which Paul calls the liberation from the old man and the gift of the new man. Jesus himself is the new man, the second Adam, the life-giving Spirit who leads us from the death of the old nature into the warm, powerful life of the new humanity. In fellowship with Him we become the salt which overcomes the decay of death. In Him we are the light which sheds life-giving warmth and guiding clarity. In Him we gain the new nature whose life-core is God himself — that new nature of the Spirit and of love.

The Sermon on the Mount brings home to us the right relationship to the Father in prayer and gives us deep trust and confidence in the Father. Jesus is the door, the narrow gateway that leads us into this life of God's nearness and God's fellowship. He frees us from the vanity and arrogance which is the underlying attitude of the man who is pious and moral in his own strength. When we stand face to face with Jesus we recognize our neediness and become beggars before God. Therefore it is an essential mark of the new righteousness that we have a longing, that our thirst for God is unquenchable and that our hunger for righteousness never ceases.

The paradox of this deepest experience of the new life in God is precisely that the awareness of utter neediness is combined with clear decision of will and genuine singleness of mind. For while the righteousness of the moralist by its very nature remains under pressure and compulsion, the better righteousness of Jesus is spontaneity.

The deeds of this better righteousness come from a life energy whose innermost nature presses to be put into action. Thus Jesus' parable of the good tree and its good fruit and the rotten tree and its bad fruits will always remain the indispensable picture by which we learn to distinguish the better justice from the worse. Only those deeds which come unforced and unintended from our inner nature should be regarded as good fruit. Our lives are lived within the better righteousness only when they bring forth the good fruit: a conduct which shows that this righteousness is completely different from any other.

The better righteousness brought by Jesus springs from fellowship with God, from the direct encounter of the soul whose life is in God. Its whole attitude reveals the Father's nature. God cannot lie; and the new justice is simple truthfulness that seeks in all things the genuine expression of its true nature. The moralistic attitude dominant in the world, the assertion of force and of rights, are now replaced by love that calls no halt even in the face of the enemy, love whose nature will not be swayed by any move of the opponent.

Love reveals itself as a vital power, a better

and stronger force that overcomes all unhealthy
degeneration of the love life and so demonstrates
purity of thought and fidelity. Because the newly
won life is built on mercy we have experienced,
the love it brings is capable of a compassion
which embraces the suffering of the whole
world. Its mercy is shown both in the capacity
to bear patiently and in the active power to
spread life and establish justice.

God's will is peace and justice. Only those
who actually do this will are within the sphere
of the new kingdom. The new life which Jesus
brings shows itself in deeds that seek love's
peace and love's justice for all men. We are
deceiving ourselves if we think that the old
righteousness of might and of standing on our
rights is the wiser conduct. Jesus compares anyone who does not act according to the better
righteousness to a foolish man whose house,
built on a poor foundation, must collapse. Only
he who hears and does what Jesus says can be
compared to a wise man who builds his house
upon a rock.

GOD OR MAMMON

"THIS IS ALWAYS the either-or: *merchant* in the swamp of commercialism, mammonism, materialism, sportism, comfortism or whatever else one wishes to call it; or *hero* on the heights of idealism. This is what God and the devil are to modern men." Thus writes Werner Sombart in his much-read war book, *Merchants and Heroes.* Jesus said, "No one can serve two masters; for either he will hate the one and love the other, or he will be devoted to the one and look down on the other. You cannot serve God and Mammon."

One of the greatest things in this great time is that this war has opened the eyes of many to see that becoming absorbed in outward things and the pursuit of money is incompatible with all higher purposes and goals, and that the great and forcible struggle of which Jesus spoke, "God or Mammon?" is still going on today.

Mamona was the Aramaic word for wealth; and it was behind this wealth that Jesus saw the true power of Satan. The latter had said even to Jesus himself, "I will give you all this if you will fall down and adore me." We cannot devote ourselves to a life of outward ease and pleasure without the value we assign to these outward things becoming the predominating force in our lives. All service of Mammon contains within it a kind of reverence or secret worship of these things, a clinging to them and a love for them that denotes a decision against God.

The attempt to combine servitude to God and servitude to Mammon must therefore repeatedly end in failure. Man with his *one* heart must love God alone and cleave to Him, but despise Mammon. God and money are the two masters between whom man has to choose; they are the two goals of living and striving that cannot be reconciled. Already in an earlier Christian period, some scholars (for instance, Gregory of Nyssa, who died after 394 A. D.) interpreted Mammon as a name of the devil Beelzebub. Others (including Nicholas of Lyra, c. 1300

A. D.) interpreted it as the name of a demon particularly connected with money in Satan's realm. The idea that the word is the name of a heathen god is a medieval fable without historical basis (see Theodor Zahn).

Here is the great antithesis. On the one side is the inclination toward bodily ease, material well-being, comfort and pleasure; the poverty-stricken view of life that is able only to *demand* from life, that wants to obtain the greatest possible amount of gain, enjoyment and ease out of life. Anyone who esteems highly the comfortable and easy life must necessarily also assign a high significance to material goods. Whoever does this must see great value in material wealth; and whoever is overwhelmed by the worth of outward things is already dominated by their power. His poverty has made him a slave because in it he wants to take and only to take, because he does not possess that wealth of life in which one wants only to give and bestow. It is the *taking* attitude to life that constitutes service to Mammon. "What can you give me, life?" is an attitude that talks only about rights; its uppermost goal in all work remains pay and gain.

It is a fact that service to Mammon, in which profit and advantage, pleasure and enjoyment are the goal of life, is an outstanding characteristic of English thinking. And it is true that all deep thinking Germans have striven toward release from this base goal of personal benefit and outward happiness. For the great German, that which is low and mean consists in everything that the masses consider an enjoyable and happy existence. For him, life is far from being a gift for his enjoyment, but rather a task.

On the other hand, honesty compels us to recognize that in the majority of the German people, rich as well as poor, the striving for money and property, for one's own benefit and advantage, for sensual happiness and comfort, has only too often repressed everything else. The German people, too, has been swept off its feet by the great flood of predominating love for things of the senses; and right in the midst of believers, love of money is shown to be the old and ever new danger which threatened even the original church community of the first Christians.

We Germans too, even we German Christians, have sufficient cause to allow the warning voices

in our country to call us to the inward goal of
liberation from Mammon. "Badness consists
precisely in loving nothing but one's own sensual well-being," Fichte once said. "You higher
people, you must overcome . . . this swarming of
ants, this wretched comfortableness which is the
happiness of the many." "It is not necessary
that I live," cried out Frederick the Great, "but
it *is* necessary that I do my duty." And Kant
summed up this striving in these well-known
words, "Duty — thou noble, great name! What
origin is worthy of thee, and where can one find
the root of thy lofty lineage? . . . It cannot be
anything less than that which raises man above
himself (as part of the world of the senses)."

Nothing but the overcoming of self, the mastering of life, is capable of getting rid of the
false, debasing life in service of Mammon; only
this can lead to a higher life. This deeper
recognition has been witnessed to even outside
the ranks of believers. Zoroaster said, "Consume
yourself in your own flame; how can you become
new unless you first turn to ashes!" And Goethe
wrote,

> *Und solang' du dies nicht hast,*
> *Dieses "Stirb und Werde,"*

Bist du nur ein trüber Gast
Auf der dunkeln Erde.

So long as thou hast not
This "die and live again,"
Art thou but a gloomy guest
Here on this dark earth.

But how is it possible to "re-become" as
the mystic Eckhart expressed it; how can one
"de-self oneself" as Goethe called it, when one
is bound and fettered as Mammon's slave? Or
how can one enter a strong man's house and
steal his goods, unless he first binds the strong
man? When a strong man who is fully armed
guards his own dwelling, his goods are in peace;
but when one stronger than he comes and
conquers him, he takes away his armor on
which he relied, and divides his spoil. Jesus is
the stronger; He has overcome, disarmed and
bound him. The cross is the triumph over the
Mammon structure built by the devil. The
victory of the cross is deliverance from the sin
of serving Mammon, from death in a debased
life. And He died for all, so that the living might
live no longer for themselves but for Him who
died for them and was raised. If we have died

with Christ, we believe that we shall also live with Him. Therefore, set your hearts on what is above, not on what is on earth. For you have died, and your life is hidden with Christ in God.

HOW CAN MEN FIGHT MAMMON?

IF LIFE IS LOVE, if love means fellowship, if all living things in their common association mold, promote and spread life, if all living things thus associated are moving toward future unity and freedom — if all this is true, then the question arises in us: How is it possible that death, destruction, mutual dispossession and murder are rampant in the world today?

In the world we know, in the epoch we live in, there is not only one power at work, the power of love and life that leads to association and to the fellowship of all. In this world and this world epoch there is also another power at work. This other power is the opposite principle. It is death that destroys life; it is separation and destruction that bursts asunder the fellowship of love. This power is a poisoning which makes the organism sick and corrupt. It is the murder and killing of life. It is the power that isolates; it is egomania. It is the power of covetousness. These powers attack radically all that holds life together at its core. These powers want to destroy the coherence of all living things. Alongside the constructive power, alongside creative energy, that which kills, murders, enslaves, and severs is at work.

Tension between opposites is the reality of our human life. When men seek to find a consecration for their lives, when they have a longing to find a devotion in this life, when men long for religion, they are faced with this either-or, with the question of God or Mammon.

It is not true when people think that everything religious is a unity and that everything irreligious belongs to the other side. It would correspond to the truth in a much deeper sense if one were to draw a dividing line of an altogether different evaluation cutting right across the religious and the nonreligious.

Everything that goes by the name of religion is related to a power that carries on its activity independently of men. The question is whether all relationships relate to the same world center, the same life content. With many who call themselves Christians and confess to the name of Jesus Christ, it is questionable whether their religion really has to do with the Father and God of the Messiah, of the coming Kingdom. The question is whether their religion is not that of the Antigod. The question is whether religion, including Christianity, is not permeated by the demonic powers of the abyss that cause the disintegration of mankind's solidarity. The question is whether the great world organization which names itself after Christ is not serving a god other than the God and Father whom Jesus confessed, the God of a totally different order. The question is whether the world church, which in practice has sided with wealth and protected it, which has sanctified Mammon, christened warships and blessed soldiers going into war, whether this church has not in essence denied Him whom it confesses with words. The question is whether the Christian state, despised as it is by the Hindus and Chinese, is not the most antidivine institution that ever existed. The question is whether a state that protects privilege and wealth as well as the organized church is not diametrically opposed to what is to come when God comes and Jesus establishes the order of justice.

We are faced here with the most revolutionary question, whether that greatest and holiest thing, reverence for church and state, does not contain within it homage to Satan; whether the justification of large landed property is not intrinsically Satanism; whether this Satanism has not led to the acme of covetousness — the murderous slaughter of fellow men. Can this Moloch possibly be identical with the God and Father of Jesus Christ? Only from the Mammon spirit do wars come; only out of the Mammon spirit does purchasable love, the defiling of bodies on the street, arise. You cannot serve God and Mammon.

It is relatively unknown that early Christianity recognized in all sharpness that the religiousness of the present world epoch is actually hostile to God. The message brought into the world by the first witnesses of the Christ was the message of God's totally different kingdom, the "transvaluation of all values." The Christians bore witness to this message of the totally different order to come, calling it the message wrapped in mystery, concealed from those who are lost, whose thoughts have been blinded by the god of this world.

Opposed to the coming God who will set up the kingdom of Jesus Christ, who will set up justice, unity and love, this God of the future, this God of the beginning and of the end, stands the interim god, the god of this world epoch. The latter is the spirit of this world, the earth spirit, brought close to us today in modern literature. This god of greed, of murderous possessiveness, of grasping and holding, is the spirit of this world. The first witnesses testified that we have not received the spirit of this world, but the Spirit that searches the depths of God, the Spirit that nobody can know unless he is known by Him.

Nobody can serve two masters. You cannot serve God and Mammon. Jesus defined with utmost sharpness the nature of this Mammon spirit. He unmasked the religiousness of the propertied classes. He showed how those who live in this sphere worship a spirit of death and murder. It is through this Mammon spirit that wars have broken out. Through this spirit, impurity becomes an object of commerce. Through the possessive will of this spirit, murder and lying become commonplace and humdrum.

Jesus called Satan the murderer from the beginning, the leader of unclean spirits. Mammon's nature is murder. Not only wars are the sign of the Mammon spirit; every day that drives hungry children and unemployed men into villages, to be chased out again by farmers with their dogs, shows us that this spirit is a spirit of murder. We have become used to numberless people being crushed to death through our affluence, just as one gets hold of a bedbug and squashes it. We have stopped thinking of the people around us who are destroyed because of us, like vermin destroyed by a ratcatcher.

We have come to a moment in history where a blind man can see that the development of the Mammon spirit means incessant murder of hundreds and thousands of people. It is because of the lying power inherent in this spirit that it is possible for the Mammon spirit, big business, to predominate. Just as we experienced during the war that lying belongs to murder as its twin sister, just as it is impossible to wage war without an inner basic mendacity — in the same way a capitalistic society can be maintained only by lying, by duping the public.

This lie is impossible to describe; nor can we go into this in greater detail here. Each individual has the duty to go into these economic problems painstakingly, to enquire into the murderous effects of Mammon and its rule. If we really turned our attention to the problem, if we saw how much injustice is common and current without the world's conscience being aroused and rising up against it, we would instantly realize the true situation. If men once recognized in a single flash that big business by nature involves injustice, their recognition would be tantamount to innermost uprising by all against the greatest deception of mankind in world history.

But we are a long way from revolting. Rich and poor must be — this is the thinking right in the midst of the most pious circles, and even among the working people. "When a man with a fortune in gold at his disposal is able to give work and livelihood to a large number of people, one must more or less put up with the situation and be glad that such an energetic personality exists." This view ignores completely

the impossibility of amassing this kind of fortune
— meaning at the same time power — without
cheating, depriving and hurting one's fellow
men and destroying their lives. This wrong
concept fails to see that since big business is
concentrated in just a few hands the decision of
one man can steer thousands and hundreds of
thousands toward certain ruin through unem-
ployment; and this is happening today.

Why do these facts remain hidden from us?
How is it possible that men are incessantly
cheated of justice and that we are blind to it?
It is because we ourselves are also under the rule
of this god Mammon.

Mammon is money ruling over people. Being
under the dominion of the money spirit ourselves, we lack the strength to rebel against the
rulership of this spirit. When life is dependent
on outward income and finances — *that* is
Mammon. Because we ourselves are completely
dependent on the income of our outward existence, because our personal lives are broken by
our own mammonism, we are not in a position
to apply the lever that lifts the slave rule of
Mammon off its hinges. Still, we are able to
recognize that money is the real enemy of God.

God or Mammon. Money or Spirit. Spirit is
the deepest relationship, the innermost fellowship of everything that is alive. Money makes all
human interrelationships venal, a matter of
buying and selling. All men have an uninter-
rupted mutual relationship with one another.
No man lives isolated. All men are interrelated
in groups, families, classes, trade unions; in
nations, states, churches, and all kinds of asso-
ciations. But not only this; through the fact of
their humanity they are also interrelated in a
much deeper way as a growing, great fellowship
of mankind.

God gives the richest relationships between
human beings, as long as the relationships
between person and person, spirit and spirit,
heart and heart, remain relationships of love
and thus lead to organic, constructive fellowship. But there is a devilish means of robbing all
relationships of spirit, of God, and switching off
the flow of heart-to-heart relationship. This
means is money.

Money converts into matter every relationship
that men have with one another. Money by-
passes relationships until finally the only value
left is money. Property and money are the means

used by the satanic power to destroy men's highest goal in life. This makes itself felt more and more as money becomes a commodity in itself instead of a means of barter; what we have then is money itself, money as *power*. Money acquires significance because many persons are connected with each other solely through money; they give up the heart-to-heart relationship and let banking take its place. Money basically excludes all true fellowship.

Money and love are mutually exclusive; money is the opposite of love, just as sexual defilement of bodies is the opposite of love; just as the killing of men in war, the murder of human beings, is the radical opposite of life, of helping love; just as lying is the opposite of love and truth.

When Mammon rules, it rules soul and spirit. It would be impossible for big business to have such power to enslave and murder but for the dominion exerted by the Mammon spirit. Under this dominion the possessive will is stronger than the will to community; the struggle for survival expressed in mutual killing is stronger than the urge to love, stronger than the spirit of mutual help; the destructive powers are stronger than the constructive powers, matter is stronger than spirit, things and circumstances stronger than God, self-assertion stronger than the spirit of love and solidarity that brings fellowship. Instead of setting men in motion and putting them to work in a creative way for the life of fellowship, the Mammon spirit has engendered an enslavement and scorn of the soul that has made us more subject to circumstances than religious man has ever been subject to God. The entire concern about the god Mammon thus becomes a deep religious searching. In truth, this spirit Mammon — the spirit of lying, of impurity, of murdering — is the spirit of death and weakness.

Jesus declared war on this spirit. He conquered this spirit of weakness by overwhelming and healing victims of sickness and death with His power. Jesus, the Prince of life, declared himself the enemy of death. He lived among us men to take away death's power, to destroy death, the devil's work. This death, the killing of life at its core, is overcome by the Spirit of life that proceeds from Christ and brings fellowship among all living things. Christ was so conscious of this that He exclaimed, "Now the judgement of this world is come; now the prince of this world shall be cast out." The Spirit will convince man that this prince is defeated.

We are now compelled to ask how Jesus conducted this fight. Did He not say, "Make friends for yourselves through unjust Mammon"? Did He not say, "Therefore give back to Caesar the things that are Caesar's"? How can we reconcile this with these other words of His: "Do not lay up treasures on earth for yourselves. . . . Woe to you who are rich. . . . Woe to you who are full. . . . And if someone sues you for your coat, give him your cloak as well"?

To examine each separate saying would lead too far afield. It must suffice to recognize the sum total of Jesus' stand. As soon as we side with Jesus we are ready to give up Mammon, to overcome it, to declare war on it. When our inmost eye has opened to the vision of His light, our eye stops reacting to Mammon's will. We can no longer gather property when our hearts are set on the new future, when we have the hope that God will establish a new kingdom. Then we shall strive only for this one thing and shall turn our backs upon everything else. We shall live for the future: freedom and unity and peace for mankind. Then the saying, "Make friends for yourselves through unjust Mammon," can be fulfilled when we give away Mammon and so gain love and make friends who will have friendship with us forever.

When that rich, pure-minded youth, who was not aware of having done anything wrong, came to Jesus, Jesus loved him at first sight and asked him whether he loved God and his neighbor. The youth thought he had done as he ought in every way. "Good," said Jesus, "If this is really so, then what you must do now is to make this love real. Go and sell everything, give it to the poor, and come with me."

The god Jesus met when He entered the sanctuary of Jewish religion was not His God, but the god Mammon: cattle and cattle dealers, banks and bankers. Jesus made a whip, not to strike people in the face, but to overturn the tables forcibly and show His contempt for money by throwing it to the floor. He testified that this house should belong not to Mammon but to God. When a spy came and showed Him a piece of money, the coin of the emperor, the head of the state, He answered, "Give to Satan what belongs to Satan, give to Caesar what belongs to Caesar and to God what belongs to God."

When someone was needed to manage the common purse on the long journey, Judas was asked to be the keeper, Judas who Jesus knew would become the betrayer. The murderer from the beginning was exposed, in the very midst of Jesus' disciples. He ended where murder must end. He disclosed the secret that Jesus knew He was the Messiah-King of the completely different order. The secret of the messiahship was betrayed. Jesus stood His ground when questioned by the political and religious authorities, "Are you the Messiah, the Son of the Highest?" He answered, "I am; you shall see the Son of man seated at the right hand of Power, and coming on the clouds of heaven to establish His kingdom." And they put Him to death on the basis of this revolutionary confession.

After this stormy attack on the mammonistic order, the Spirit-born community was seemingly destroyed; for its leader had been killed and eliminated. In the religious and irreligious alike, the power of money seemed to triumph; the will of Mammon, the will of death seemed to have the upper hand in the end.

Yet through the very execution of the leader of this new order, through the grave itself, life won out. Amazingly, from this downtrodden people, the Jews, young men and a few young women meet to wait together for the completely new. They wait for the Spirit. They know that this spirit of love, of order, of freedom is the spirit of God's kingdom. The Spirit comes upon them. Here is an example, a church, a fellowship of work and goods in which everything belongs to all and all are active to the full extent of their varied powers and gifts.

And yet this church succumbed to the deadly process that destroys life. Just as individuals die, so this church also died. But in the course of the centuries a new church rose from death. Time and again small communities were formed in which men and women together declared war on Mammon and together took upon themselves the poverty of generosity. In actual fact they went the richest way by choosing this poverty of generosity. People filled with this urge of love can be found throughout the cen-

turies. We hear their voices, we join hands with
them across the centuries. We feel a fellowship
of faith with them, faith for the future.

God has demonstrated that He did not die;
but the Mammon spirit has shown that it too
is at work. God is waging a crucial war against
death, against Mammon. The God of Jesus
Christ is the God who today is not yet God over
all things. He is the God who is on the way. He
is the God who will prove that He lives when
His kingdom dawns, when history reaches the
goal of all goals. He is the end where everything
finds its fulfilment. He is the protest against that
which dies and murders; He is the rebuke
to everything in us that lusts and robs and
grasps. He is the conqueror who clears out the
robbers' den, who brings judgment over all men
that covet possessions and property. In his-
toric protest He has revolted against perverted
humankind.

Among primitive peoples we find a simple
communism. In later periods the revolutionary
struggle, the fight of the Spirit against materialism, continued as a vital issue throughout
history. We who witness the appalling results of

capitalism today stand at the point where the uprising against capitalism begins. The goal is the overcoming of private property, that is, socialization; and there is no doubt that we are moving toward this goal with certainty.

We are on the same side as all revolutionaries who assault the champions of Mammon. We belong with them and they with us. He who is not against me is on my side. He who is not on my side is against me. These words of Jesus hold true for us.

There are two ways, both committed to the fight against Mammon. One is the way of Socialism and Communism. The other way is the new way of communal work and fellowship in things spiritual and material; it is voluntary, independent gathering together by people who are free of private property and capital. This way is the organic growth of the germ cell, the way of the seed that sprouts right in a stony field. Here and there a little tip of grass shows through. After a few days have passed and sun and rain have kissed these grass tips, you can lie on the ground and see a great field of living tips; and again a few weeks later, you will see a whole field of flourishing life. Though weeds and stones be there, the young crop will break through. What the individual blade of grass cannot achieve, the whole field can. Harvest time is here. Pray that laborers may be sent out into the harvest.

Before the harvest, wheat and weeds cannot be separated. If bloody revolution hangs the servants of Mammon on the lampposts, so that only people of the community spirit may be left, [this is completely against the spirit of Jesus.] You should have waited until harvest time; you have torn out wheat as well and left grass standing. There are still covetous men left who say, "Now it is our turn to take away the rights of others." We cannot put our trust in such words. Such words lack the Spirit to whom we have to give witness through Christ. If by bloody revolution Mammon passes into the hands of others, if today we have to hear of our brothers being shot by the Bolshevist government because they have given witness to the unity of men, we take our stand with these brothers.

We have no part in violent revolution. Just because it sheds blood, it is on the side of the father of lies. Our brothers lie to themselves if they think they can overcome Mammon by physical violence; for violence is the same spirit of the abyss as Mammon itself. Only of the new can the new be born. We cannot drive out poison by means of poison. Only out of life comes life. Only of love can love be born. Only out of the will to community can community arise.

Our way to the goal of community is that second way. We walk the communal way of brotherliness where small bands of people shall meet, ready to be merged in the one goal, to belong to the one future.

Already now we can live in the power of this future. Already now we can shape our lives in the presence of the coming God, in accordance with the future kingdom. The victory of the Spirit manifests itself through the church community. The mammonless kingdom of love is approaching this earth. The kingdom of God has come very close. Change your thinking radically. Change radically, so that you will be ready for the coming order of things.

> Next a word to you who have great possessions. Weep and wail over the miserable fate descending on you. Your

riches have rotted; your fine clothes are moth-eaten; your silver and gold have rusted away, and their very rust will be evidence against you and consume your flesh like fire. You have piled up wealth in an age that is near its close. The wages you never paid to the men who mowed your fields are loud against you, and the outcry of the reapers has reached the ears of the Lord of Hosts. You have lived on earth in wanton luxury, fattening yourselves like cattle — and the day for slaughter has come. You have condemned the innocent and murdered him; he offers no resistance.

Be patient, my brothers, until the Lord comes.

GOD MAMMON AND THE LIVING GOD

A THREEFOLD MESSAGE to guide men to true life on earth: truth, purity, and work on the land. This was the message given to men by the Persian prophet Zoroaster of old.

This leading thinker recognized, however, that there is another force opposing the tremendous power of truth, purity, and work, and the fellowship of love that arises from this trinity. He realized that two opposing powers are active in this world. Zoroaster was the first prophet to express this recognition so powerfully outside Judaic prophecy. But the two powers of opposing tension he speaks of are not inseparably divided worlds, such as this world and the otherworld, or spirit and matter, as in modern dualistic thinking. Instead he sees these powers in the tension of two opposing poles which challenge each other: good and evil, life and death, light and darkness, the antithesis of obscurity and clarity, the contrast of day and night. He wants to expose in all its force the struggle between the good power and the evil power in this world.

Every evening that the sun sets; every night that it grows darker and darker and the moon conquers the deep blue darkness of the starry heavens; every morning that the morning star rises to herald the coming of the sun; every new day born of the night; the birth and death of light, and in a very special way the waning moon which eventually becomes only the white-grey ash of the dark-gleaming new moon and yet becomes once more the radiant full moon — all this points to the mystery of the marvelous victory won by light over darkness, by good over evil.

Zoroaster's words, preserved till this day, give us a clear direction here.

> God creates spirit,
> spirit gives truth,
> truth gives freedom,
> freedom gives faith.
> God says: I will be with you.

And there are you,
born of selfishness,
spirits of evil
and prophets thereof,
and thou the first among them —
glittering lies!
Your deeds are the same;
they are known
in all the earth's regions.
You have your power
by flattering men,
lulling them by things pleasant,
so they tire of work on themselves
and stagger away
from God and from his duty.

You call this life?
Of true life this is death!
With your worldliness
you rob men of eternity.
But this is what evil wants;
it wants annihilation.
On a thousand ways it lurks;
thou alone, God, knowest them all.
The better and the evil shall end;
then what was good shall emerge.

a chaos of sound.
There are those who remember
their loyalty to thee;
they cling to thee and call out to thee.
The others forget what thou gavest;
they leave thee and cry treason.
But to those who still waver,
thoughts move from one to the other,
speaking in secrecy.

But alas, Lord,
I am in the midst of them.
Therefore I ask thee:
How is it to be,
now and for all the future?
Is the good which is done
and the evil which happens
written down as in a book
for a final reckoning?
This I ask thee:
How shall it not be forgotten
that the wicked man is helped
to do violence;
that people feed themselves
by pillaging men,
animals, and the land?

This I ask thee:
whether in goodness there really is
a possibility for action;
whether cunning is not the thing
which really counts in this world?
Yes, O my God,
does this not appear the only way
to reach the goal?
At sight of this world
I would oft cry out:
Can it really be that truth is the better,
when there is so much lying;
and must I not join
in their howling?

God, do not forsake me.
Make me strong in this trial.
Give me strength.
Down with thee, O rebellious thought;
the sword at thy throat!
For look well:
Does this bring inward peace
over home and community,
over country and world?
Is the deepest life healed
by craving for outward things?

Only he who knows
from which source life springs
can draw from the eternal well,
and only this refreshment is true comfort.
Sparks once flew,
and there will be a flame again.
The better and the evil,
two sticks that rub each other;
but the fire is good, only good!

Step here or there,
be smoke or flame,
be crushed, suffocating in smoke,
be raised up in flames!
There are you, yours is the choice!
But know that you do not choose
between God and the evil one.
As long as you still have to choose
you know nothing of him yet.
For God is higher and deeper.
He gives constantly
a world which never perishes,
the secure peace of truth,
the peace of his spirit.

Whoever tries to follow these ancient words will feel what a tremendous struggle comes to expression here, and that any superficial separation and distinction between people becomes impossible. There are many who believe that religious people, the idealists, the devout, stand on the one side in this struggle, while materialists, those concerned with outward things, are found on the other side. Certainly, this provisional classification of mankind has a certain human psychological significance, but it does not go to the bottom of the matter. Basically it misses the point.

The great struggle going on is a struggle that takes place in the heart of every materialist just as much as in that of every idealistic or religious person. It is a struggle that goes on in mankind and in man himself, and we cannot say that the good people are to be found on the one side and the bad people on the other. It is not true that the religious life is good and that the materialistic life is bad. The important thing is to explore and to recognize where materialistic thinking puts its faith and where religious life finds its god, where the spirit of each is found, and what the object of veneration is for each.

There is, in religion as well as in atheism, an Antigod whom we can worship as our god. Early Christianity was filled with the conviction that there is a god in the world who is not the God of Jesus Christ. There is a god of godless, worldly religion, in opposition to the life Jesus led; a god of the present era, in opposition to God's future and God's eternity.

The nature of the Antigod is work without soul, business without love, machinery without connecting spirit, craving for possessions without mutual help; it is lust instead of joy, destruction of competitors, idolization of private property through fraud and deception. This god is not a god of goodness. He is not the God of love. He is not a god of fellowship. He is not the God of the future, not the Father of Jesus, not the one who will bring the coming order of justice. No, he is an interim god of the present age of history. He is not a god of loftiness and light, but a god of the abyss, a spirit of darkness. He is a fiend of enormous power, one who corrupts everything, one who brings death, one who embodies the power of evil.

This mighty demon of our age cannot simply be identified with superstition. Superstition is part of his nature, but only a part. He does incorporate superstitious belief in the power of numbers and days; in the power of fear and of outward things; superstitious belief in the autonomous, sovereign, demonic power of every isolated area of life and domain of influence. Yet his power extends far beyond these spheres. Not only does this anti-divine spirit create the superstitious notion that makes soldiers wear an amulet around their necks so that while committing murder they will not be murdered themselves. Not only does this spirit cause specific conjuring charms to be used in exorcising evil spirits while the user of them is himself possessed by these spirits. This abyss, this demonic, satanic, evil power operates even in the most religious place, just where religion wears its best appearance and its most pious mask.

We read in the writings of early Christianity that a god of this world epoch has blinded the minds of those who cannot believe, of those who perish; it has corrupted their vision, so that they are no longer able to see what really matters or to grasp the message of the future, which is the message of liberation, of mankind's coming unity, of the coming God. The spirit of this world epoch is a spirit not of God; therefore it cannot see the purity and truth of His future. It cannot recognize the deep things of God, yet it is a spirit eager to penetrate the depths and to understand deep things. It is concerned with the deep things of Satan; it wants to know evil by actual experience; it seeks friendship with death and its weapons; it seeks to explore all vices and passions. It is the deadly spirit of paralyzing intoxication and suggestion which brings the illusion of power without the strengthening of true power. It is a spirit that brings weakness, a spirit whose power means weakening. Jesus once laid His hand upon a woman suffering from a nervous disease which bent her body and utterly weakened her life. Jesus said of this woman that Satan had bound her and that she had to be set free from these bonds.

This spirit of darkness is the spirit of weakness, the spirit of death, the spirit of disintegration, the spirit of murder. We all know the effects of this spirit from personal experience. The experience of being redeemed and liberated from this spirit makes one much

more deeply aware of the deadly atmosphere
from which he has escaped. Therefore the
early Christian writing says the following about
this former existence of those who are now freed
and brought to life: "We were dead through
trespasses following the course of this world
epoch, following the prince who has power in
our atmosphere, following the spirit that is now
at work in the people of disobedience." Not until
the spell is already beginning to break do we
first glimpse how powerfully the atmosphere of
this spirit controls us all and holds us in its grip.

We are all so closely and firmly bound up with
this exceedingly mighty spirit of death that we
become incapable of discerning clearly its dangerous nature. We do not have the perspective
necessary to recognize and evaluate its character
clearly. This is why we need the guidance of
a serene, pure spirit of truth, to be able to
recognize the nature of this spirit of our age by
specific characteristics.

This spirit is the spirit of fashion, not only the
fashion of the moment, but the spirit of fashion
and style of this entire epoch in which we all are
placed from birth on. It can become completely
unmasked and overcome only when a new age, a

coming era, shall put an end to it, the death, the covetousness of all ages.

Already the resplendent star of the world's coming day has risen; Jesus has opened warfare on this spirit. Jesus could do this as the leader of the coming age. Zoroaster, the ancient Persian — and deeper and clearer than he, the prophets of pre-Christian Judaism — already foretold this mighty struggle which Jesus was to inaugurate. They painted in all the colors of faith their glowing optimism for the radiant future of this victory of good over evil. Victory presupposes warfare, presupposes the clear demarcation of the opposing front lines. Jesus was speaking of the same struggle, the same certainty of victory, when He said, "You cannot serve two masters. You cannot serve God and Mammon." He puts him in opposition to God as an antigod.

We would not be able to understand the words, "the god Mammon," unless we knew the other terms by which Jesus exposes the nature of this spirit. He calls him the murderer from the beginning; He calls him the father of lies, and He calls his spirits the unclean spirits. Jesus, like Zoroaster, demands truth, purity, and love. The other spirit stands in opposition to this trinity. The nature of this spirit is mammonism. Its trade is murder, its character lying, its countenance impurity.

To the moralist, these traits are four completely different things that have nothing to do with each other. Yet for all who can see more deeply there is no fundamental difference between these four things. Mammonism is covetous will, will to seize, possess, and enjoy. The impure and murderous spirit is covetous will, out to corrupt the life of others through possession and pleasure and for the sake of possession and pleasure. It does this either through the suggestion that the other life is obstructing one's own possession and pleasure, or else by inducing the intoxication of lust, by which the hedonist enhances and intensifies his own life and increases his own power while corrupting the life of another, which he seizes and possesses for his own pleasure. A man then becomes a twofold murderer by the same covetous will that governs Mammon. And lying — the expression of spineless character, the fraud of a life that is disunited within itself — is the consequence of the same covetous will.

We simply cannot bring anything into fellowship with covetous will. Yet we must live in fellowship; for we are dependent on associating with others as long as we want to participate in life. And if we are possessed by the covetous, murderous spirit of mammonism and unbridled sexual lust, we will have to tell lies every time we are together with other people.

We have to tell lies in business, in the effort to hide the greed of our mammonism, the selfishness of our endeavors, the materialistic motives of our human contacts. We are forced to show ourselves differently from what we are; for no fellow human would associate with a money-greedy beast of prey. Nobody would want to have anything to do with a hyena that lives on the corpses of others. So the filthy wolf has to don the white fleece of the lamb; the sly hyena has to put on the sheep's mask of the solid citizen. The old fox has to feign innocence; business chicanery has to be done in the most inoffensive-looking way.

Lying must serve, then, in all the great wars of every nation, in all the great revolutions of class war everywhere. For the weapons of truth and clarity cannot possibly be used to defend covetousness and selfishness or make them victorious. This dishonest state of affairs proves more clearly than anything else that trust and unselfishness are indispensable, that dedication and will to fellowship are absolutely necessary in all of life's activities. Ethical, communal motives must at least be simulated just to be able to survive. In reality these motives, good though weak, are usually combined in an unclarified, dirty mixture with the purely selfish push for power and craving for pleasure.

This is the only explanation for the "honest" appearance of the businessman who destroys his competitors and takes advantage of his clients. It is the only explanation for the highly moral motivation of the destruction of all wars, including civil wars; for every ruthless act of state that deliberately dispossesses and harms other nations. It alone explains the patronizing exploitation, the oppression and starving, of employees by their employers. For the perceptive, this lying is the clearest proof of the truth which it simulates.

The same is true of the impure spirits that arise everywhere out of the deep abyss of covetousness. Impurity is impure in its lying nature. Unfaithfulness in sex relations is the profoundest and meanest deception imaginable. It is the killing of the soul by deceit and trickery. Nowhere is there so much lying as in "love," where real love is feigned for the sake of enjoying, abusing, and corrupting without restraint.

This makes it clear that these apparently different designations — Mammon, lying, murder, and impurity — disclose one and the same spirit, one and the same "god."

Once we have recognized this and now look at the reality around us, we will be constantly amazed about the enormous power this god possesses in the great world. We will be more and more deeply frightened by the words of Jesus summoning us to battle: No man can serve two masters. You cannot serve God and Mammon. This means a great deal. Lay up no treasure for yourself on earth. Sell all that you have and give to the poor, and come, go the completely different way with me.

It seems impossible to break these chains. Wealth works as a curse because it stands in the way of liberation. It is an affliction because it

burdens. It is a woe because it satiates but
cannot fulfil. Woe to you that are rich, woe to
you that are full. Blessed are you that are poor.
Property kills friendship and motivates injustice.
There must be a great turning point, when
friendship will be won by giving away Mammon, when fellowship will be found by turning
away from injustice. Make friends for yourselves
through unjust Mammon. Win the friendship
of hearts by giving away and surrendering all
the goods of Mammon you may own. Go the
new way, the way of community given by the
Spirit. Enter into fellowship with men. Seek the
unity which, coming from God, penetrates
through the soul right into material things.
Away from Mammon! Turn to God!

On hearing the word "Mammon" we first
think simply of money. And indeed, money,
tangible money that we can hold in our hand,
is the most characteristic symbol of mammonism. Mammon means wealth to begin with; it
means attributing a high value to money; it
means the converting of human relationships
into material values.

All men live in relationship to one another.
The child is borne by his mother. Father,

mother, brothers, and sisters guide him into life. At school he grows up in the companionship of his classmates. Later, the young person enters the work relationship with fellow workers. He finds an ever-widening view and understanding of his responsibilities in life, of how he can build up the common life in the fellowship of service with other people.

Love enters the life of the young person. In the experience of a great joy, a deep happiness, two people become one in faithfulness, sharing their life and their material possessions. In them and through them the tremendous being and coming-into-being of life community begins its new cycle.

Just as it is in the life of the individual, so it also is in the life of all, in the great nations, the great collective classes, the great social units: nothing exists alone, by itself. No age, no century, not even an instant in time, stands by itself; everything is related to something else. The more living these relationships are, the fuller and richer is life.

Naturally, this relationship can also be one of opposition, even of strife. And strife, too, is a living relationship. Often the honest adversary is the best friend. We often come closer to each other's hearts in an open, clear fight than in an indifferent, superficial, and fleeting relationship.

Love your enemies. This is not only an enormous demand. It also powerfully embraces and joyfully affirms the lives closest to us in the most personal way. Except for my friends, my enemies are closest to me. It is with them that I have to come to terms most frequently, in my thoughts and actions, but most of all in my emotions. Hence it is my enemies, no less than my friends, in relation to whom I have to prove the strength of my inner feelings. I cannot be indifferent to them; I must concern myself with them in the most intensive way. Since I cannot avoid doing this, the question is in what spirit this intensive occupation will be strongest and most fruitful. What will be the deepest concern, the most powerful and living relationship to them that I must find? The best relationship, in reality the only possible one, is that I love. Only in this way will my relationship to my enemies be fruitful. "When I hate I rob myself of something, but when I love I become richer by the object of my love." (Schiller)

Life is relationship and reciprocity. Everything is constant giving and receiving, constant coming and going, constant reaching out to one another, and daily working hand in hand. Men are called to a fellowship of feeling, a fellowship of work, which must become enduring. They are called to a fellowship of emotion and will, a fellowship of knowledge and creative work, a fellowship of faith and hope, a fellowship from heart to heart. They are called to fellowship of life.

But here is money, the mightiest empire in the present world order — gold, that stifles and obstructs this fellowship. Everything among men which otherwise would be living interchange and devoted service and mutual help here becomes a thing, a coin, a piece of paper. Not that the invention of money as such is evil. What is evil is the way this dust that is money swallows up what is living in man's spirit, and therefore in the contact of men with one another. This, then, is the satanic nature of money: that in our lives we have financial relationships to one another, which no longer are personal relationships, which no longer are a fellowship of faith and life.

In our civilization we observe relationships

whereby men buy one another and pay for one another. Human strength is paid for and consumed by men. There is no fellowship between these people. Because of money, men are no longer valued as human beings, but valued and treated as a commodity. It is not surprising, therefore, that in the traffic of goods there is even less of a living relationship between those who produce and sell the goods and those who receive and use them. Commodities are received and paid for without concern for those who produce or sell them. Personal labor and service rendered has gone into the money used in payment, work either done by the one who pays or done for him by another, whom he may neither know nor care about.

Because of money, people forget the exchange of work done and service rendered. What takes its place in our mutual relationships is a materializing, a converting of the spirit of fellowship into something that is no longer fellowship, but its opposite. From this results the soul-killing custom of buying, or receiving money for services, of employing and paying for labor, without any community between the receiver and the giver. Wherever and whenever this happens we have fallen prey to Mammon, to Satan. All these business and labor relations, impersonal and devoid of spirit, are built essentially and principally on money. They are mammonism. In this we see a truly ghastly development of our present-day civilization.

Today it is practically impossible for an employer in a giant factory to have a contact with all the workers with whom he has a clearly defined labor relationship expressed in terms of money, and to carry this contact on his heart. With the shareholders in a joint stock company this becomes absolutely impossible. Here the mutual relationship of the investors themselves to those who do the real work has been completely eliminated. The meeting of shareholders, the company meeting, the board of directors, and the management are pushed in between investor and worker. There is no one who is responsible in the personal sense for what happens to the worker. The shareholder or shareholders can always refer to the management and board of directors, and the board of directors and management can always point out that they are responsible to the investors. There is no way for the working masses to establish a relationship

with their employers through their work. All
this has been displaced by the inaccessible stock
company and its drive for efficiency.

Here we see the roots of the soullessness of
modern industry. This can be seen most clearly
in the bookkeeping system, where cash account
and payroll statistics are all that really matters.
Here money alone—a number—counts; hence
the working human being, too, counts only as a
number — a payroll number, a profit statistic.
Everything personal, everything that creates
fellowship, has been eliminated from the process
of production. This is characteristic of the
whole machine system. The soul is not admitted
into the factory. It is handed over at the time
clock. In return the worker receives his number
from the time clock and has to function as
part of the huge machine. His work is controlled
by machines and instruments, and in this way
the production schedule is enforced.

The much admired Henry Ford has achieved
the very utmost in this soul-killing enslavement
to dead machinery, enslavement to the principle
of automatic profit on investment. This industrial magnate has robbed work of its soul, of
any mental or technical accomplishment, to

such an extent that seventy-nine percent of all operations in his industrial plants can be performed by completely unskilled labor. Forty-three percent of the production requires only one day of work training, another thirty-six percent requires only eight days. Hence only twenty-one percent of all workers, mechanics, and foremen are allowed to put into these famous Ford cars even a little thinking of their own, a little workmanlike skill of their own. The great majority, the other seventy-nine percent, are imprisoned during their working hours as soulless slaves, sacrificed to capitalist profit and condemned to a humdrum existence.

Another widespread system, called the Taylor system after its American inventor, is equally soul-destroying. For the purpose of making the highest possible profits, the whole work program is painstakingly and rigidly regulated by exact rules and norms. Thus not even the merest stirring of a person or soul toward free decision can slip through this tight mesh during the strictly controlled work hours.

Everyone who gives some thought to this can find hundreds of other examples in all spheres of life of how money and profit kill the soul and make fellowship in work more and more impossible. We will recognize in the most diverse instances that money, originally intended as a means of exchange, a harmless facility in the mutual exchange of services and the fruits of labor, has turned into the accursed Mammon. Mammon, symbolized by money, has become the all-subduing power agent. It works in covetousness that clings to money; in judging things by money, thus devaluating the soul; in transforming human relationships into something material, into money, which prevents and annuls all heart-to-heart relationship between men.

Hence the counter-symbol of a Francis of Assisi — voluntary poverty and the complete relinquishing of money — is needed again and again, especially in our present age of large-scale capitalism. Usually people react with indignation to those who, for the sake of love and freedom, refuse to touch money. This very reaction shows us that Mammon—the deluding power of money — can be abolished only by such a step into the economically impossible. Certainly, both money and the abolishing of money are but symbols, though powerful ones, for what is real and essential behind them.

God Mammon is not merely the same as money or private property, though it is true that these are overcome by the Spirit. The God of the coming kingdom of love is not found by simply doing without money or having common property, although He will bring these things about too. Mammon is in communism as well as in capitalism. For the old-school Marxist and many of the dispossessed, the need for food, clothing, housing, everything economic, is the mainspring in history, the only force that drives men. In the struggle for existence, they say, the class war of the have-nots against the haves must be waged to the end; our whole life is a material one and arises automatically out of this basic urge to exist, out of the instincts of self-preservation and reproduction. This way of thinking is again mammonism. For if we build our mutual relationships only on the requirements of food, clothing, shelter and sex, then we are again basing these relationships on a materializing of the spirit.

Yet in the protest that arises from Marxism there lives a great, deep truth. For what the movement for social democracy basically strives for is not the economic interpretation of history. It is not materialism; nor is it "surplus value" (the difference between wages paid a worker and the value of his work). It is not the idea of automatic transition from capitalism to socialist state enterprise via the trusts. And certainly it is not the idea of collective economy as such. No, the ultimate driving force of this movement is faith in a future of justice, faith in the victory of light, faith in a fellowship among men which will extend to material things as well because it will embrace absolutely everything. The ultimate, hidden force behind this materialism is the revolt of the spirit in the name of matter; it is a universal mass attack on the mammonism of the "spiritual" men who have the Spirit on their lips but desire what is material.

Conversely, the materializing of relationships through money can be overcome in the propertied classes too, by hearts united in brotherliness, administering goods justly for the benefit of all. Faith in the future, the ultimate future of justice, can be alive among capitalists; it can be alive in materialistic socialists; for it can live in the heart that seeks love and believes in a just future. If we feel this, then we can be convinced,

like the Persian Zoroaster, that there is a power
of good which is stronger at all times and in all
places than the force of mammonism.

In our world this faith seems impossible.
What moves and shakes us most deeply in
Zoroaster's verses is that even in him the doubt
arises whether after all evil and cunning will not
finally gain the upper hand in this world. But
again and again he fights through to the faith:
No, ultimately the spirit with the greatest power
must triumph. The greatest power is the light,
which is truth and purity and active dedication.
The greatest power is love.

This prophetic certainty of love is the prophetic hope of early Christianity and the Old
Testament. God is creative power. God is the
Spirit. God is love. God is truth and clarity.
This God is the God of the future. He has a goal
on this earth, and this goal means justice and
peace; it means the overcoming of mammonism,
the spirit of lying, murder, and impurity. God's
future is the victory of truth and purity; it is the
victory of the creative spirit of justice and love
over unjust Mammon.

Jesus took up the fight against this spirit of
Mammon in the certain faith that He is the

victor who will vanquish this mighty, dark spirit. However, we must get rid of an old misunderstanding, the idea that the kingdom Jesus proclaimed is purely otherworldly; that His intention was to make good one day in heaven everything that is and will always remain bad on earth. Then we would have to become people of the otherworld, people who long above all for the hour of our death, people like Trappist monks who lie down daily in their coffins so as to be wholly prepared for dying. To die would then be man's true liberation. Death would then be the redeemer, giving us the final kiss to free us from the shackles of this shameful existence. Then by death we would be lifted out of this accursed bodily life, this pseudo-reality, into a paradise of spirits, a paradise of pure, bodiless joys.

This concept is widespread not only in Buddhism but also in Christianity. It must be emphatically rejected. What was said for Zoroaster in the beginning must be affirmed just as strongly and yet in quite a different way for Jesus. The great division between God and the devil is not the division between the life here and the life beyond, between matter and spirit, between corporeality and incorporeality. On the contrary, this division runs right through all spirits and all bodies, through all eternities and all times. In every house both spirits are at work in full force. In every body, every human being, both powers are working; both forces operate in every age, in every moment of history, including this one now.

The decisive question is this alone: In what way will the Spirit, the only Spirit of life, come to rule in each person, in each moment of time, in each body, and hence throughout the whole planet Earth? And how will Mammon, the earth spirit of covetous will and injustice now ruling, be conquered and eliminated?

Mammonism exterminates the fellowship of all that is living. It is the enemy of life. It is death. The kiss of death is not the kiss of the liberator. It is the pestilential breath of the ravager. Death is the last enemy to be conquered. Death is not our beloved brother whom we embrace because we are fond of him. Death is the enemy whom we must trample underfoot as quickly as possible. Whatever leads to death, whatever pushes men out of life and living fellowship in mutual dedication, whatever ruins health and beauty in life, is of the devil.

Brothers, love the earth. Brothers, be true to the earth, and do not believe those seducers who look longingly at the otherworld so as to cast suspicion on this world. Jesus is the greatest friend of the earth — Jesus who again and again, in the original spirit of Judaism, proclaimed love for this earth, love for the soil, love for the land. Blessed are the peacemakers. They shall have the land.

In Zoroaster's writing we find the startling combination of truth, purity, and work on the land, made as the basic demand and promise of divine life. In Jesus and the prophets of Judaism we find that their proclamation of God's coming kingdom testifies to the same miracle of "spirit and land" that comes from God. God, the Spirit of love and justice, of purity and truth, will come; this creative rulership will burst in upon this earth and bring the new earthly regime. This earth shall become the land and garden of a justice and joy, a truth and purity of mutual relationship, such that only then will the true God-ordained joy of life begin on this planet. The earth shall be conquered for a new kingdom, a new order, a new unity, a new joy in true community.

This is the message Jesus brings. Jesus has the certitude that this message can be believed today, that we can live in accordance with it today. Seek first and last this kingdom of the new order coming from God. Seek God's future, God's coming. All the other things, the things on which the spirit of Mammon wants to build up life, should not be the object of your concern. Your outward, day-by-day living will be given at the right time. What matters is the new order, the transforming and new creating of all things and all circumstances. When new men are begotten of the Spirit, when they are born anew as the new life from God, these new men will then tread underfoot the unjust devil of Mammon, of murder, lying, impurity. As free men they shall stride across into the new life. Already now they shall and must proclaim and live the new kingdom.

It is not a matter of a future utopia flashing up infinitely far off. On the contrary, already now the certainty of this future is present power. This God who will bring the future onto this earth lives today. This Spirit who will bring about the unity of all men is alive today.

This unity is reality today. Mammonism is overcome because this power has appeared in Christ. Whoever believes in His coming and in the victory of His Spirit — very simply, whoever believes in Christ — can know His power here and now, can make the decision of faith here and now to renounce unjust Mammon, to let his own covetous will die, to stop telling lies, to stop taking part in murderous acts and desiring what is impure.

The secret of this fellowship of faith in the future is that it is happy in love without being covetous in lust. The mystery of this expectation of the future is that already now it puts to work the love for all men which slumbers in every human heart. This love then acts in the simplest work on the land, with the soil, in field and garden, but also in all other manual work and all mental work.

In every human being there lives the same divine spark that breaks forth jubilantly from the idealist German poet, Schiller, when in his *Ode to Joy* he writes of the brotherly love that embraces the millions of the whole world. From the starry firmament, from the Father of all love, the spirit of the future is bestowed; it gives eternal life to that love which embraces all, that love which is living deed, devoted, steady work, which fulfills life in sacrificing it.

Basically this is something so simple, so clear and so plain. It is joy in everything that lives. Anyone who can rejoice in his fellow living beings, who can have joy in people, in their spirit and in their lives, in their fellowship of nascent church community, anyone who feels joy in the mutual living relationships of trust and inner fellowship — *he* experiences what love is.

Anyone who cannot feel joy cannot live. Love is born of joy. Love and the justice of love only dwell where there is joy. The spirit of joy is what we need to overcome the gloomy spirit of covetousness, the spirit of unjust Mammon and its hate that kills. Such joy we can only have if we have faith, only if the earth and mankind once more become for us something that has a future, because it is from God. Hope must arise new, the great hope which is ultimate certainty.

Once during a meeting of socialists, independents, and communists, the leaders challenged the worn-out, tired workers to close ranks once more in resolute firmness for the solidarity of their union. We asked these leaders and the whole assembly, "What is the use of all such calls for common action, for the heroic courage to pull out of deadly exhaustion after certain defeat, unless first this question is answered: Is the faith in a just future still alive in the proletariat? — the faith that the unjust distribution of the necessities of life will be overcome, and a just and peaceful fellowship of work will arise among men? Is this faith alive or is it not? Only if it is alive can there be solidarity. If it is not alive there will be none." All had to admit that this was the crucial question. Certainly, they felt that this faith had been wounded and weakened among the workers; but, though flagging, it could not be killed. All were unanimous that this faith could not die.

There is one thing that should unite the most contrasting political factions and the most divided Christian and non-Christian confessions, however sharply and openly they stress their differences. That is the inner certainty that everything must and shall be completely different; the inner certainty that what is bad, what destroys fellowship, what kills and bursts apart, what shatters trust and cleaves asunder, will be eliminated and overcome; that in its place the joy of love, the fellowship of justice, will be victorious.

This faith is not something purely spiritual that helps us to acquiesce in unjust conditions. This faith is the strength of a reality which relates to material things just as much as to mind and spirit. This faith is ultimate reality. It is from God — from the God without whom there is no reality because He is the working cause of all reality; He himself is creative life. This faith is the certainty that unjust, murderous, divisive Mammon will be overcome by the loving, the living, the all-uniting God.

The distribution of land and work, of all goods in life, should be in harmony with the justice of the God who lets the sun shine and the rain fall on just and unjust alike. As Jesus says so simply, this love gives itself to all men. Whatever you want that people should do to you, do the same for all others. Fight to obtain for your fellowmen, your brothers and sisters, the same things that you need for your own health and well-being, to be able to do for mankind the task entrusted to you.

Let us unite. Let us be one. Let us go to all men. Together let us win community in all things for all. To become men we must be brothers. To be brothers we must be men. To become a community we must come alive. There is only one living brotherhood — brotherhood through faith. There is only one faith — the faith which believes in everything that overcomes death. Faith is faith in the living God.

THE DECISION

ONE OF THE MOST dangerous and widespread errors is the belief that everything that is at all religious has to do with the same God, that everything religious goes forth from the same God who is the God and Father of our Lord Jesus Christ. Jesus and the early church of the apostles discerned connections and opened up abysses here of which most people who call themselves Christians have no inkling, no concept.

The apostles of early Christian times expressed this by saying that there is a god of this world and that the god of this world is a completely different one from the God and Father of our Lord Jesus Christ. They spoke of a god of this world who does his mischief in the hearts of unbelievers and blinds their senses and their eyes so that they cannot perceive the brightness of the gospel, the true message from God and His Son. They speak of a spirit that rules in this world and possesses this world. Jesus spoke of a prince of this world, or ruler of this earth.

A contemporary drama, frighteningly bestial and true, speaks of the earth spirit and portrays this earth spirit as the devil of sensuality and the Mammon spirit of this earth. In essence this strikes at the truth. Much that we call Christian is anti-Christian; much that we call divine is anti-divine; much that we call religious is religious precisely in the religion of this other spirit and other god that is opposed to the God and Father of our Lord Jesus Christ.

In wonderful clarity and glorious lucidity, Jesus named and unmasked the being of this prince, this earth spirit, this god of the world. He chose four designations to make thoroughly clear to us how sharply the god of this world stands opposed to His God, the God and Father of Jesus Christ.

First He calls him the father of lies from the beginning; second, He calls him the murderer from the beginning; third, He calls him

Mammon; and fourth, He describes him in his unclean spirits as the spirit of impurity. In these four designations lies hidden the ultimate antithesis which the god of this world wants to hide from the God and Father of Jesus Christ. He is not the Father of Jesus, who is the truth; he is the father of lies. Wherever lies dominate, wherever untruth rules, wherever religious untruthfulness prevails, it is important for us to recognize that what we have here is not Jesus and His God and Father, but the god of this world, the spirit that controls the children of unbelief, the prince of the abyss, Satan.

Lying in any form comes from below; and most terrifying of all is the religious lie. It discloses the nature of hell. Closely allied with this lie is man's disposition to murder. Think of the World War and the newspapers during the war; or think of the revolutionary struggles and the newspapers of that time, and you will see that everywhere the lying spirit and the murderous disposition are indissolubly bound to one another. This spirit of murdering is the spirit of the devil. Every spirit that is out to kill other people comes from below. Every spirit that untruthfully belittles the opponent, that is silent about all that is good in his nature and exaggerates the bad, comes from below, from the father of lies, the murderer from the beginning. The World War and the revolution have shown us that this lying, murderous disposition is in indissoluble partnership and connection with impurity of atmosphere.

We do not want to speak today about life behind the front and the sin there, or the confusions of war, the marital unfaithfulness at home. Let us think only of the present. Let each one be reminded of himself and each one of us become clear about himself, that unchastity in life is inseparably bound up with lying and the spirit of murder and crime.

Because of shaking things experienced in friendships with seeking persons, I am constantly aware that lying and impurity and murder are inextricably joined together in one and the same action and experience. An army officer had broken down. He did not know how to break with his mistress. He was held in fear of the woman who shared the common guilt with him by actions he had done with this

unhappy person, actions intended to prevent
further consequences and disclosure, actions that
could bring him to justice and public prosecu-
tion; for she could at any time betray him and
ruin him. Because of the murder of incipient
life which he had on his conscience, he felt
himself forced to drag along the unbearable
burden of his impure life. Fear of punishment
forced him to continue in this lying life, a
broken man, close to madness.

These three shaking forces of the abyss —
lying, impurity, and murder — which unfold
such a sinister power in the present day, are
comprised in a fourth power which we commonly overlook. This is the spirit of Mammon.

Without the Mammon spirit there would be
no war. Because of the Mammon spirit, love is
purchasable and bodies are thrown into the
gutter and besmirched. Because of the Mammon spirit, lying is carried to extremes — the
lying that people do to each other in business,
in the contacts between whole classes, in the
exchange between nations. You cannot serve
God and Mammon. Mammon is domination
by money; it is the dependence of life on
material income and financial circumstances.

Mammon is the overriding relationship to money and property.

Human beings live in continuous mutual relationship. They never live alone, but always in groups, families, tribes, and nations, and ultimately as one single growing, great fellowship of this earth. Between these human beings the richest and most manifold relationships exist, relationships created by God as long as they are relationships between person and person, from heart to heart, relationships of love, which lead to the organic building up of fellowship.

Opposed to these relationships of people to each other, however, there are diabolical ways of breaking off entirely the personal, the relationship of heart to heart. The most important of these means is property and money.

Money is the materialization of men's relationships to one another. It has become so all the more strongly since from being a means of barter it has become a commodity, a possession in itself. Money is the relationship that exists between many people who do not want to come close to one another or who believe it is impossible for them to have a heart-to-heart contact.

Money, with its materializing effect, with its mammonistic spirit that excludes true fellowship, is the exclusive opposite of love — the true relationship between men — just as much as sexual defilement of bodies is the opposite of love, as war and the murderous spirit is the opposite of love and as lying is the opposite of love and truth. The will to possess is stronger than the will to fellowship. The struggle to survive is stronger than the urge to love.

The Mammon spirit is the control of human beings by *things* instead of by the spirit of love for persons and for fellowship. The Mammon spirit is dependence on circumstances and conditions in the place of dependence on God. The Mammon spirit hardens the heart in egoism; it comes from self-love instead of from the spirit that lives for others and gives itself for others.

We realize, then, that it is impossible to serve God and Mammon at the same time. It is an either-or decision. If we are dependent on God and love God, the God and Father of Jesus Christ, then we become people of love, remaining in heart-to-heart contact with people; then we become like the God of love, in that we overcome the disposition to murder

and try not to injure anyone's livelihood. If we
are people who love God, we are people of
purity; then we are free of the filthy impurity
that drags love into the dirt and into hell. Or
else we are people of Mammon and in our
relationship with people we consider only how
much money we earn, what advantages we
have, how we can be successful, how to enlarge
our property, how to make our living secure,
how we can overcome financial worry by accumulating money. By doing this we harden the
love in our hearts; we corrupt the truthfulness
of our innermost longing toward God and
toward love; we also corrupt radically the
deepest urges of our love including that of man
for woman and woman for man.

This great decision, then, is the ultimate
decision in each person's life. It is the decision
between hell and heaven, and it is the decision
between the Creator in His Holy Spirit of love
and the degenerate creature in his defiled body,
his final corruption. It is the decision between
God and devil.

Once a wealthy young man came to Jesus. In
the heart of this young man Jesus saw so much
longing for the good and pure, for the genuine
and true, for the divine and loving, that He

loved him at first sight. And this young man was
in fact a man of noble traditions and trustworthy morals; he was a man who had religious
feeling and who wanted to learn from Jesus. So
he asked Him, "Teacher, what good deed shall
I do so that I may have eternal life?" After he
had claimed that he had killed no one, that he
had never committed adultery, never stolen or
given false witness; yes, after he had claimed
that he honored father and mother and loved his
neighbor as himself, Jesus pointed out to him
the untruth of this claim. For he had *not* loved
his neighbor as himself. Jesus said to him, "If
you want to be perfect, go and sell what you
possess, give it to the poor, and you will have
treasure in heaven; and come, and follow me."
When the young man heard this he went away
in sorrow; for he had many possessions. And
Jesus said to His disciples, "Truly, I tell you, a
rich man will find it hard to enter the kingdom
of heaven. Also I tell you, it is easier for a camel
to go through a needle's eye than for a rich man
to enter God's kingdom." When His disciples
heard this they were astonished and said, "Then
who can be saved?" But Jesus looked at them
and said to them, "With men this is impossible,
but with God all things are possible."

The rich youth had believed that he loved his neighbor as himself, and Jesus wanted to lead him into the deepest truth, to show him whether it was really true that he loved his neighbor as himself. The youth valued his property and the ease and comfort of his outward existence. Now the Lord was saying to him, "You love your neighbor as yourself; then I will tell you how you can be perfect. If you love your neighbor as yourself, you will wish for him the same conditions that you have, the same luxury and comfort that is given to you. If you wish to be perfect, go, sell what you have and give to the poor and follow me." Then the young man went away sorrowful.

Jesus loved this man and wanted to win him. There is not the slightest doubt in my mind that Jesus really wanted him as a disciple, and perhaps this rich young man might have become a personality of outstanding significance like John, James or Paul. But he could not be detached from overvaluating material things, from servitude to Mammon. To this young man, Mammon meant more than God. The spirit from the abyss, the spirit of dependence on outward circumstances, was worth more to him than the Spirit from the heights, the spirit of dependence on God the Father of our Lord Jesus Christ.

This story is of exceptional importance for our time. Of course, it does not mean that everybody should now be obliged by law to sell his investments, to dispose of his goods, to give up his business and then divide the money among the poor of the city. The point is that Jesus tries to show by a thoroughly clear, irrefutable example that conversion to Jesus and to God must mean full and radical separation from Mammon, from money.

The point here is not whether we give up our property. The point is that we do no less in any area of life than what is demanded here; that we surrender our money and our life so completely to God that we will be ready — whether today or tomorrow — to sell our fields and our goods, to give up our business, our investments, our bank book, to give our everything to the Lord and to the poor. The important thing is that we turn radically and completely away from money and its influence; that money no longer can dictate to us; and that we devote ourselves fully with all our income, all our money and our talents, to God and His will to love. The important thing is that we do not regulate our relationships with other people by the Mammon spirit, but that we turn our backs on money completely and regulate our lives solely by relationships of love and the spirit of love that God, the Father of our Lord Jesus Christ, creates in us.

It is significant that Jesus ever anew brings about examples such as those He brought about here. It is of importance that He gave us a Francis of Assisi. This man came from a wealthy family and was under the influence of Jesus. He realized that he was vacillating between love for God and love for money, between love for his neighbor and love for himself. Then one day he went into the woods and there, in a lonely chapel, he heard the story of the rich young man; and he was converted to God. He returned to his home town, sold his possessions, his splendid clothing, his horses and carriages. He dressed like the simplest folk and went wandering from village to village, from town to town, just to preach Jesus and to do His deeds of love.

In modern times God has brought about similar examples. In a book by Karl Joseph Friedrich, *The Empress' Poor Sister,* there is a story that brings these problems very close to our hearts in narrative form. It is the story of a man in Russia. He too was from a wealthy family. From his childhood on, God would not let him go, and he received deep impressions of Jesus. One day his heart was struck by the story of the rich young man and his decision; he sold everything he had and wandered from village to village. Wherever he went, he lived in the love of God. He did not care about holding long sermons everywhere; what he cared about was to serve and to help in the spirit of Jesus. Where a poor woman was ill, he would help her. Where a yard was dirty, he would set-to and improve it. Soon he became the most beloved and revered person in every district through which he passed. But the cross came to him too. The Spirit urged him to protest everywhere against the religious lying of his people. And so it came about that, after working with wonderful effectiveness, he was finally thrown into prison. There he was tormented, until he collapsed completely. But the witness of this man is still having its effect today. And just as his passing was a childlike one — the world would say one of childish joy — so his witness is a call to wander, to wander in the discipleship of Jesus, to serve with devotion in His love and to turn from Mammon to God.

To mention a different example, I know of a wealthy man who possessed large factories and had millions at his disposal. And I know that this man was so unpretentious in his person that his suits and the overcoat he wore for many years attracted attention because they were so threadbare, worn and crude. He kept his enterprises and did not give his property away all at once. However, he did not use this wealth for himself, but administered every penny of it with great conscientiousness and unpretentiousness for God alone, for Christ and His gospel alone.

God sends such examples into different times and peoples so that we may see what the difference between Mammon and God means, what decision and conversion from Mammon to God means.

It would be a great mistake to think that only those who are in control of large sums of money are in danger from the Mammon spirit. Jesus shows us that there are two alternative forms of mammonism. These two possibilities do not depend on our will; the movement of heart is the same in both cases. They simply depend on the destiny God has given us. One person expresses the Mammon spirit — love of money and material things — by accumulating treasures and wealth, while another expresses the same Mammon spirit, the same dependence on outward things and servitude to them, by worry and care.

As long as grey care rules in our house, it is not the Spirit of Jesus Christ that prevails there. As long as grey care spreads out its dark shadow over us like a spell, a curse, and we are not freed from its gloom, the sun of Jesus Christ and the love of the Father has not dawned upon our hearts and our lives. As long as worry holds our hearts and our lives in its imprisoning spell, we are on Mammon's side and not on God's side. We can see that this worry and the need that goes with it brings about all the sin we have heard about, sin in the direction of the Mammon spirit.

After last night's meeting an unhappy young

girl came here to talk. This young girl had had
a good position in Berlin. A seducer came to her
and said, "Come to Hamburg, give up your
position; you will have it much better there."
And when she had gone to Hamburg, he said
to her, "Give me a hundred marks out of your
salary." But she obtained no work in Hamburg
and therefore had no salary; and he left her
and went away. Now worry was in her heart,
and worry threw her onto the streets and into
the gutter. Worry brought her to selling and
defiling her body night after night.

It is worry that produces class hatred in us. It
is worry that causes us to grit our teeth and
clench our fists whenever we see a car or a
carriage passing by. It is worry that makes
secret triumph arise in our hearts when the
blood of the rich is shed, that calls forth hatred
and envy and generates murderous feelings in
us. It is worry that entices us into lying in
everything we do, whether we are poor or rich,
whether avaricious and money-greedy or full of
worry and vassalage and fear.

If we are not at home in the fatherly arms of
the loving God, if we have not come home to
God and the Father of our Saviour Jesus Christ,

we are all the "purchased slaves" of the prince of this world, the spirit of the abyss, Mammon, the father of lies, the murderer from the beginning and his impure spirit. There is but one deliverance from this need: Seek first God's kingdom and His righteousness, and all these things shall be yours as well. "Believe in God and believe in me," Jesus cries out to us. Believe that God is greater than all money and all outward circumstances; believe that God can sustain you like the flowers in the field and the birds on the roofs. Believe that God can clothe you with great splendor, for He loves men as the crown of His creation. Believe that God wants to redeem you from outward trouble and fear, from inward worry and fear.

We feel with you; we know the kind of lying in which you have found yourselves or may find yourselves today. I was cut off from my parents' house for some time, and I experienced God's wonderful help in a time of severe need. My wife and I have from time to time told with amusement of how a servant girl once overheard me praying alone to God, "God, send us...," and I named a definite sum of money. This girl wrote home that the Arnolds were on the point

of bankruptcy. Dr. Arnold was already praying
for money, and probably there would soon be
something about it in the newspaper. However,
nothing appeared in the newspaper; instead,
· God sent the money we needed, just as we have
often experienced receiving from God what we
requested for ourselves and our work, our needs,
without having to turn to people. We have
learned that God cares for us as He does for the
birds and the flowers. Every one of us can have
this experience, can learn this secret. It only
depends on our daring to make the plunge into
the freedom of the living God and the kingdom
of God as Jesus revealed it. His kingly rulership
in our hearts — that *is* the freedom we need.

Mammon is not overcome by diabolical lying
and murder. We are glad that revolutionary
movements protest against the Mammon spirit.
We are glad for every protest against devilish
mammonism. But at the same time we feel
very deep pain; for we see that undeniably the
slavery of the Mammon spirit is active in these
movements, expressing itself in murder and
lying and all kinds of impurity.

There is but one deliverance from the spirit

of Mammon, from the devil of impurity, from the devil of lying and of murder, and that is Jesus Christ. Jesus Christ overcame the abyss on His cross. He founded the kingdom of God. He drove out demons through the Spirit from God, and by doing so He proved that God's kingdom has come to us. Whoever accepts Jesus today, whoever of us receives Jesus' Spirit in his heart, will find and experience that all evil spirits will leave his heart. It depends simply on the question, is there a spirit stronger than the spirit of lying? Is there a spirit stronger than the spirit of impurity, the spirit of hate, the spirit of Mammon? This is the question that decides your destiny for time and eternity, your hell for today and your hell for eternity.

We are here to witness quite simply to a reality. There is a Spirit that is in fact stronger than the spirit of lying, stronger than the spirit of impurity, stronger than the spirit of hate, stronger than the spirit of Mammon. It is the Spirit of Jesus Christ and His God. Whoever receives Jesus Christ in his heart, whoever becomes one with Jesus in his soul, conquers all the forces of darkness. He has the victory over the devilish powers.

One day Jesus shall come and establish in His authority His kingdom of peace, of joy and justice, on this earth. He shall drive the spirit of murder and hate, the spirit of Mammon, out of mankind and out of the earth. This is our hope. And our experience is that already today we have God's kingdom in Jesus Christ, as justice and peace and joy in the Holy Spirit.

The Lord is the Spirit, and where the Spirit of the Lord is, there is freedom.

RESISTANCE BY SURRENDER

THE PERFECT PEACE which appeared in Jesus Christ and His church must, in accordance with the true prediction of prophecy, be attacked by all the powers of world economy and by all national governments with their sharpest and deadliest forces. Glowing all the more surely and clearly, the character of unconditional peace delivers its bearers defenseless to the flaming sword of their opponents. Jesus' Sermon on the Mount presents the sharpest prophecy of the kingdom of peace: readiness to suffer every death, which is the resistance of the will to peace. Against the peace-breaking violence of the whole world it puts up the passive resistance of the cross. The cross against the sword!

The cross is the radicalism of love. The peace of the Sermon on the Mount attacks things at their roots. It gives away to love the last remnants of possession, down to shirt, coat and cloak. The will to peace gives its whole working strength, undivided, to the total, fully united communality. As often as love commands, willingness to sacrifice will quietly double the distance or the working time asked.

The church of peace carries on without letup an active, creative general strike against the whole injustice of public unpeace that surrounds it. In this break with the whole status quo, Jesus recognizes no justified or justifiable claims or rights. He does not allow His church to take legal action. He does not let it take part in trials. He commands it to omit or interrupt any religious exercises whenever brotherly concord demands this, whenever the honesty of brotherly unity is in question. He opposes the dishonest cult of disunited piousness by upholding and restoring the unity of love.

Jesus' Sermon on the Mount gives the unconditional command and all-inclusive authority never to offer the slightest resistance to the power of evil. This is the only way the evil one can be made good. Jesus' will to love would rather be struck twice than return a single blow.

Love surpasses all things. It admits of no other emotion. In marriage too it stays faithful and combats any separation or divorce. Love permeates hidden prayer as forgiveness. It determines public conduct when the will for total reconciliation is absolute, embracing even the enemy — yes, him in particular. Rather than ever returning cursing and hatred, injury and enmity, whether singly or collectively, it never takes the slightest part in hostility, quarreling, or war.

Love is not influenced by any hostile power. The attitude of Jesus or His follower cannot be changed by any turn in a situation. No matter what happens, he only *loves*, he practices only *peace*; he wishes, requests, and does only good. Where the peace of Jesus Christ dwells, war dies away, weapons melt, and hostility dissolves. In Jesus, love became boundless; it became sovereign.

Here at last the justice of which the prophets spoke materializes fully. The justice of Jesus Christ is better than that of all moralists and theologians, better than that of all socialists, communists, and pacifists. For in it flows the sap of the living plantation of total future peace. Here the strength of salt, God's innermost essence, is at work. Here the light from God's heart shines out as the beacon fire of the city on the hill whose towers proclaim freedom, unity, and surrender. Here each one wills and does for *all* whatever he desires for himself. Here no one gathers a fortune of his own. Here no heart grows cold in icy fear and worry about one's own economic survival. Here rules the peace of love.

Here all citizens are unswervingly concentrated on the *one* goal — God's will and God's rule, God's heart and God's being. Here none stands opposed to another. No one is condemned. Nothing is forced upon anyone. No one is despised. No one is violated. And yet love reigns as truth. Yet the nature of the inner heart can be recognized by its fruit in deeds.

All see clearly that such a resolute common will provokes the keenest antagonism on all sides. The bond of full unity that joins and gathers is taken as a provocation. Felt as hostility to mankind, as maddening exclusiveness, it excites the indignation of those who, like the

masses, are neither able nor willing to accept
the call of such complete fellowship. Conflict is
unavoidable. No one can escape it.

This living fellowship of hearts, in a firmly
welded bond of all working forces and material
goods, stands out in thorough contrast to the
conduct of the whole world. This necessarily
causes particular bitterness in quarters where
people are being recruited for deeds of violence
that are justified in ideological terms. For here
every hostile action is rejected outright, no
matter what weighty justification is found for
it. All participation in warlike, police or
juridical proceedings is excluded, no matter how
plausibly it is justified on the grounds of
protecting the good. Nor can one have anything
to do with violent uprisings, even though they
seem necessary in the name of oppressed justice.
The very existence and nature of this symbolic
life provokes to combat all, right or left, who
think that government by force is the highest
duty of the hour.

God is unchangeable. His name is "I am who
I am." His heart enfolds everything and remains
the same for all. In Jesus Christ His heart was

revealed. Jesus Christ is today and forever the same as He was in all His words and deeds. What He is now and here is the same as what He shall reveal himself to be in His kingdom.

The words of His love point the same way for all things. What He said for the future members of His kingdom holds true for all His followers at all times. Everything He said for them is all of a piece, just as the sap of a tree, the strength of salt and the flame of light are *one*.

Therefore Jesus' words about marriage cannot be taken out of the context of the Sermon on the Mount. Jesus represented the will of love, expressed as the will to unity, in marriage. But He represented this just as much in nonpossession, nonviolence, and nonprivilege; in freedom from judging, in forgiveness, and loving one's enemies.

Poverty that arises from love protects one from a bad conscience, because it does not allow of injustice, as the ancient Ecclesiastes testified. Love that is complete presses on to voluntary poverty, because it cannot keep for itself anything that a neighbor lacks. Love makes defenseless, because it has given up self-preservation and knows nothing of revenge.

It remains undaunted and for conscience' sake bears evil and wrong. For, like Peter, it remembers Jesus' Sermon on the Mount and knows that this dauntless stand is God's greatest gift, because it shows His heart. Nonviolent firmness discloses the love that overcomes all.

Love foregoes everything of its own. Anyone who by a clear conscience protects the mystery of his faith will stay away from any dealings with legal or hostile actions, just as the elders of the early church did. The justice of Christ will not sue. It does not act as intermediary. It does no business to the disadvantage of its neighbor. It abandons all advantage, sacrifices every privilege, and never defends a right. This justice will not sit on any jury, take away anyone's freedom or pass a death sentence. It knows no enemies and will not fight anyone. It will not go to war against any nation or kill any human being.

And yet this justice is the most active in work, in peace, in constructiveness. The sum total of all we are commanded to do is love — love with pure heart, clear conscience and unadulterated faith. Where there is perfect love, Jesus gave free course to the conscience responsibly living in fellowship with God, in the essence of His kingdom and His church.

The love called agape — this is Jesus' way. His love tolerates no unclearness. This love is unique. It gives a very definite direction. It is a way; and this way is marked out very distinctly. Through the experience of God's love, Jesus Christ leads up to the highest and purest peak of will power, clear understanding, and the heart's strength which is joy. He does not do this for our sake. He wants us to pass on the streams of this power of love that is poured into our hearts. They must flood the earth. They must conquer the land. They shall disclose God's heart. They shall establish God's honor.

His heart is His honor. It is *love*. It turns toward all men in the joy of giving. Love is God's honor. His justice is love. To strive solely and exclusively for God's kingdom and His justice brings about in us such a love for all men that we want the same for them in all things as we want for ourselves. This alone is justice, to give up our lives for love.

Nothing but the whole Christ, for the whole of life, will change and renew everything. Half of Jesus for half of life is a delusion, a lie. The spirit of life will not tolerate a selection of guiding principles or elements of faith such as a self-willed spirit tries to pick out for itself from God's truth. Truth is indivisible. Christ cannot be dissected. Whoever does not try in all matters to take the same stand that Jesus established in wholeness and integrity has rejected Him. No justification, no matter how clever, for his half-hearted behavior, will shield him from the judgment, "Whoever is not with me is against me."

There are some who, while they want to hear and read and learn this, that or the other about Him, at the same time have a way of obliterating everything that seems to them impossible by weakening it with explanations. They, together with their whole life, though it appear ever so Christian, will collapse. Jesus says that all who hear His words in the Sermon on the Mount but do not do them are like those who build on a shifting foundation. What they build is lost from the outset. It succumbs to the first attack of hostile forces.

Christ, who is whole, wants us whole. He

loves decisiveness. He loves His enemies more
than His half-hearted friends. He hates His
falsifiers more than His opposites. What He
abhors is the lukewarm, the colorless grey, the
twilight, the foggy, pious talking that mixes
everything up and commits one to nothing. He
sweeps all that away whenever He draws near.

He comes to us as He is. He penetrates us
with His whole Word. He reveals himself to
our hearts in His wholeness, His completeness.
In His coming we feel all the power of His love
and all the strength of His life. Everything else
is deception and lying. Jesus Christ never comes
close to anyone in a few hasty, transitory
impressions. Either He brings the whole kingdom of God for ever or He gives nothing. Only
those who are willing to receive Him, complete
and for ever, can experience Him. To them it
is given to know the secret of God's kingdom.
To all others He veils himself in enigmatic
metaphors. Anyone who stops short of a full
surrender hears parables without understanding
the thing they point to. With seeing eyes, he
sees nothing. With hearing ears, he understands
nothing. Whoever does not want to have everything will lose the little that he thinks he has.

True life is the all-inclusive awareness that is able to see deeply into the reality of things and events and at the same time to see far out into the distance. It bears the world's suffering. It hungers after justice. For it has heart; it is heart. It is God's heart.

God's heart appeared in Jesus; and to God's heart Jesus consecrates the future. All those who in Christ believe in the future of God's heart are from now on committed to the total will for peace, at any time, in any place.

The first requests of the Lord's Prayer, then, speak for the innermost desire of Jesus' closest circle, the peace prophecy of the Old Covenant which shall restore the final and absolute: the name — the will — the kingdom!

The dawn of the new time lights up the invisible city of peace. The hidden land of fellowship rises into view. In the Holy Spirit of the church, the new Jerusalem comes down. It is the city of perfection, the city without a temple; it has done away with cult. Its life in fellowship *is* the great King's temple of peace.

The church bears the sevenfold light of the

sabbath of peace, when man's own work shall
rest for ever because God's great work has
begun in quiet. The city of peace and joy opens
up the brilliance of the new creation. The first
things have passed. The last enter with power.
Everything becomes new.

The present world can see in the church
community an image of the city of peace. This
image is a signpost to the future. All must see
it. Not a corner of the earth can be left in the
dark. The light held aloft penetrates all spaces.
The city of light sends forth light-bearers. The
life fellowship of the city on the hill is identical
with the life of traveling and mission.

New birth is the narrow gate to the kingdom
of peace. Inner peace is seen as liberation —
freeing from dark sin, release from the curse.
Birth sets eyes on the light of the new world.
God's kingdom is visible.

The more the abrupt contrast between one's
own weakness and helplessness on the one hand,
and the power and glory now beheld on the
other hand, is seen to be the contrast between
man and God, the more forcefully does the new

emerge. God's cause takes the place of man and his suffering.

The peace of the coming kingdom brings forgiveness of disruption and sin, and harmony with God's power of love. All the forces of a will hitherto dissipated are from now on directed in new, previously unknown clarity to God and His kingdom. Just as one learns in wartime to feel the blessings of peace, so too, peace of heart depends on the powerful contrast to sin and disharmony, weakness and disruption. Life is possible only through this tension between man's fragmented powerlessness and the energy of God's peace.

The center for the new people is the new hearth of the new church; around it their communal dwelling place arises. Around the radiating fire of the Holy Spirit their spiritual temple is built up as a tangible house of God. This is the city on the hill whose light beams out into all lands. This place of worship burns in spirit; it shines in truth.

The fire of the Holy Spirit brings the church above, the church of glorified martyrs, down to the throng of believers gathered around Christ's flaming throne. In the flame of the Spirit there is living unity between those who have passed on and those who remain on earth. The unanimity of the people gathered for full community in the house of God is the unity of the church above; it lives in that perfect light to which no mortal life on our shadowy earth has access.

The glowing love of the perfect spirit of unity takes its leading from the city above. Not only does it lead the believers, weak people as they are, to community of goods in food, land, and all things. Not only does it bring them to fellowship in all their work. It guides them to pass on the flame through hospitality and fire-bearing mission, serving as messengers to all men over the whole earth. The unity of the church becomes the light-kingdom's message of peace for all the world.

The Spirit is the mystery of the city on the hill. Apart from the one way — the way of the Spirit that gives unity with the city above — there is no city below. Outside of this there is no church. The city church of God lives only in the pure air of its eternal mountain peak. Its citizens and their politics are of heaven. From there this city expects everything. From there it is ruled.

THE SPIRIT OF LIFE OVERCOMES

THERE ARE PEOPLE who, in spite of their earnest inner efforts for their subjective religiousness and orthodoxy, are not yet overwhelmed by the unique Spirit of Jesus Christ. These people do not belong to the church community of Jesus Christ or to the mission. This is an extremely painful fact for many. For the only way they know to help themselves is to try honestly to love other people and to see to their own salvation. But these people do not belong to God's kingdom. This is terribly frightening, but it is the truth.

Only the chosen, the sought out, the elect, belong to God's kingdom and Jesus Christ's church community — those who by the imparting of God's grace have received the spirit that is wholly different. This is the spirit that does not strive for one's own holiness, one's own salvation; that does not try to make oneself good and to make oneself out to be good. It is the spirit that recognizes and honors God alone and God's interest alone.

This is a mystery which Jesus expressed only in parables, with the sole exception of the Sermon on the Mount, where He said directly and literally what it is that counts. The Sermon on the Mount shows us a tree that God plants, a sap in the tree that our blood cannot produce, a salt that we cannot manufacture, but whose nature is given by God. It shows us a light that we cannot kindle; an essence that comes to us, never from our human sources, but from the fount of God's being alone.

The Sermon on the Mount contains a mystery that has been utterly impossible for many of its advocates to understand, including Tolstoy. No new set of laws is given here, no five new commandments or prohibitions are laid down here in the place of the old Ten Commandments. What is revealed here is the new tree, the new light, the new salt, the new essence; this is God's heart which came to men in Jesus Christ and attains dominion in the coming Kingdom.

The Lord's Prayer, the prayer to God, is therefore the central focus of this new light. That His kingdom come, that His rule break in, that His being be revealed and honored in His name, that His will be done as it can be done only through God — this is the call to God in the Sermon on the Mount. Planted into this call is the whole gospel. It is the request for daily bread, both spiritual and temporal. It is the assurance of forgiveness of sin. It is the freeing of the whole earth from all the devil's might and force. It is protection in the hour of temptation that is to come over the earth.

Here is the demand for human action and human decision, set into the midst of the Sermon on the Mount: Your inner eye must change! The inmost vision of your most hidden being must be changed. Until now you have only been seeing cross-eyed. Your inward eye has been looking in all different directions at once. Different desires and concerns animated you at each moment. Never have you been capable of concentrating on the one single thing and being true to this one thing. But now your vision must become concentric; your inner eye must become single. You must become completely simple, completely resolute for the one, the only — God's kingdom and His justice.

Thus you must not have property. You must not gather wealth; for that would divert your eye from God's rule and God's justice. But you must not have worries either; the spirit of worry about your livelihood, about the little details of food, clothing and shelter must never make you its slaves. You must not be the kind of people who are tyrannized by grey Dame Care. Freedom from possession is the necessary demand of this one spirit, this pure spirit that wants and intends God's rulership and its justice and nothing else. You ought to be so free from these material things and objects that you feel like the flowers that are clothed out of the creation, doing nothing for their clothing themselves; so free that you become like the birds that receive their nourishment from the creation, neither planting nor sowing, neither ploughing nor tilling.

Only the one who immerses himself completely in God and His command is capable of finding this freedom from possession and from the spirit of care. And he also becomes truly free from the conditions and circumstances that prevail today. For him it makes no difference what the juristic court proceedings agree and decide upon, for he does not go to law. For him the words, "Do not judge!" are a decision against all legal institutions. He definitely would rather take off his coat and cloak and shirt than begin a quarrel about anything outward. He clearly would prefer giving up his nighttime hours for work to ever refusing anyone's request to go a short way or reach out a helping hand. He goes far out of his way to meet his opponent or enemy or those who seem to be his enemies, so as not to allow a spark of the hostile judging fire to penetrate his own heart. It is clear to him that the single heart, the gathered and concentrated vision allows of no exaggerated words, no swearing of oaths, including those sworn before authorities or courts. He knows that here is the completely simple, completely plain truthfulness that says what is necessary without idle phrases or rhetoric and says nothing beyond what is necessary nor less than that.

This spirit gives the clarity that makes it impossible for hostility and enmity to arise here in the region of God's kingdom. Here there is love for all opponents. Here is winning love, perfect love. Here is the love that through the inward glow of the heart draws everything into the sphere of love. Therefore the way evil is combated here is not by resisting it forcibly, but instead by not allowing evil's principles and practices to find their way into life's struggle.

Here evil is combated only by means of good, through love. Thus in the realm of human love as well, full clarity must rule. No unfaithfulness in human relationships can arise here. Here no greed for variety prompted by lustful desire can take root. Instead, the singleness of resolute hearts must be proven, the unity of two in Christ-centered marriage. Then any covetousness that makes the eye look sideways is recognized as out-and-out sin and done away with.

This is the secret of an attitude that knows but one law — perfect, pure, true love, manifested in all areas of life. This is the Sermon on the Mount.

For this very reason, however, Jesus in this talk distinquishes in the sharpest way between the different spirits. This attitude has nothing of the soft-mindedness that could say yes to everything; for that would mean at the same time saying no to everything. It is a completely clear yes to that which alone is important, to God's kingdom and His justice, and therefore a clear no to all other endeavors. Test the spirits! By their works, by their fruits you will recognize them. It is the deeds that determine the spirit. It is not what a man says and asserts that determines the spirit that dwells in him; only what he does and what his practical work is like discloses which cause he serves.

There are two animals in creation that show us the crucial contrast. The wolf shows us the sneaking nature of the beast of prey. The lamb shows us readiness for sacrifice, gathering, solidarity and spirit of sacrifice in the group. All works must be tested as to whether they demonstrate the nature of the beast of prey that lusts and lacerates, that wants to possess and to kill, or the nature of the lamb that holds together and stands ready for sacrifice. The lamb's nature knows what serves the whole flock.

In the Sermon on the Mount Jesus sums up the call to go through the narrow gate, on the narrow path, in this watchword: Behave to men as you wish them to behave toward you. Strive to attain for all men whatever you struggle to get for yourselves, whether for your nature, for your natural requirements — the physical necessities of life — or for the needs of your soul and spirit — the inner necessities of life. That is the small gateway, the narrow path. In whatever you do, think of all. Whatever you achieve, achieve it for all. This alone is the way of Jesus Christ. We must act according to these words. If anyone does not act in this way, the structure of his life will topple in ruins. But anyone who does act by them will build on rock; for he lives from the sap of life from God, from the Spirit of Jesus Christ. That is the way we are called to go.

Let us not become anxious! Let us not be cowardly! We will not slacken our efforts, but be courageous. With the greatest courage let us take reality as it is. And it simply remains a reality here on this earth that a band of human children is sure to have many, many imperfections, shortcomings and weaknesses and to lack gifts in all possible areas. Anyone who knows anything at all about human life must realize soberly and objectively at the outset that it just cannot be otherwise.

The first thing, then, is that we cannot make

superhuman demands of one another, for that is unfair. It would lead us into a legalistic, moralistic way whereby those who have the gift of order push aside and despise the others. This evil spirit of hostility and arrogance is the greatest enemy; we must thoroughly reject and banish it from our midst. We must gain the humility, the courage to be small, knowing precisely that even if a person has more gifts in this or that area, the same person perhaps has fewer gifts in another area. We need to be able to bear one another in love and in daily forgiveness. Otherwise community is impossible. For no group of human beings will ever come together that has gifts so perfectly attuned to one another that no conflicts due to human weakness would be possible. Never and nowhere is there such a thing on this earth.

That is the first thing. But the second is equally important. We must never lose our faith as a result of our sober insight into these conditions; for that would mean losing everything. It is our faith that the Holy Spirit, who penetrates our inmost being, also wants to bring what is most outward and material under His rule. It is our faith that the boundary line between the one and the other cannot be found in the distinction between spirit and matter or between depth of faith and material work. It is our faith that this boundary line passes right through the spiritual as well as the material, through economy and finance as well as through Christianity and piety.

It is our faith that material objects and work arrangements are fully mastered by the innermost spirit of perfect peace and perfect unity. They are fully mastered in the sense of this spirit, though with the limitation I mentioned before; this full mastering is limited by the lack of gifts of those human beings who are working together. But as far as the Spirit is concerned, as far as God is concerned, this penetration is complete. To the extent that we believe the Spirit and allow the spirit of faith to penetrate us, the care of material things and the building up of the cause to serve as many people as possible will be complete. To the extent that the Holy Spirit rules in our work as in our lives, the church of Jesus Christ will give a true picture of God's kingdom, including the outward aspect of material things and work arrangements. And only to the extent that human peculiarities, the accursed human stubbornness and the regrettable human weakness and lack of gifts — in so far as these come to the fore the picture will be imperfect.

It is just as Paul says in the seventh chapter of the Letter to the Romans. Who will set me free from this body of death? I am not able to do what I would so much like to do. Again and again I do the evil I do not want to do at all. In myself as a human being I can find no good. But after the seventh chapter comes the eighth; and here suddenly we read that there can be no condemnation for those who are in Christ Jesus. No judgment can be carried out on them, for that which is born of God overcomes the world. The life law of the Spirit in Christ Jesus has set me free from the natural law of sin and death.

According to this eighth chapter, then, there is a situation in which the spirit of life overcomes and rules and has control of earthly and material nature, which is subject to the natural law of death. We must believe in this. But it can take place only through the spirit of humility and love, for that is the Spirit of Jesus Christ. It can take place only if we, together with groaning creation, direct our sight toward the

end, so that the dazzling splendor of the
throne of God's kingdom is seen, so that the
redemption and deliverance of the sons of God
shines out over the whole of creation. And this
is just why the church is given — to dare to
start *now* with this future world, so that that
which will be perfect in the future world of
God's kingdom may now begin.

The same apostle says this again in a different passage. God's kingdom already now
consists in justice, in peace and joy; it exists
through the Holy Spirit. The will to perfect
love depends on faith in the Holy Spirit, the
faith that the Holy Spirit will, in spite of our
human weakness, fill our hearts with glowing
love and penetrate and conquer and form all
working materials and all human relationships
and creative powers in the work.

In short, the first secret of the Sermon on the
Mount, the singleness of the inner eye, the
simplicity of the concentric vision, must become
manifest in the practical life itself. So we want
to attain extreme simplicity in all our daily ways,
the greatest simplicity humanly possible. Simplicity of form, simple clarity of conduct, simple
poverty with liberation from the gathering of all

treasures — this is the goal. The more plainly and simply we give shape to our work, and the more simply the lines of our work are seen, the more we shall reveal the true picture of God's kingdom and of its deepest meaning.

Objects must not be allowed to tyrannize us, or we would be lost. We must place them in the hands of the Holy Spirit; then all objects will be fitted together in such a way as to show a picture of ultimate simplicity in all our work. Then we will also be placed in a position where by simplifying our life we can serve all the more people, the more faithfully we can care for all objects in this most sacred sense of love and devote their use to all those still to come.

Jesus prayed, not only for those who were entrusted to Him, but also for all those who were still to be won in the future by the word of the apostles. Thus our daily work must be protected in such a way that everything we do is a prayer, a loving prayer for all those who may come to the church even years later, through the witness of our work, and be provided by the church with shelter, clothing and food. In everything we do, love must lead us to do this: Whatever you expect for yourselves from the community, do the same for all others, including the many who are still to come in the future!

If we are newly gathered together in the full unanimity of this simple loving spirit, all conflict among us will be resolved. Then we will be able to give one another the greeting of "peace and unity" with courage and joy. Then we will not need to fear the political persecutions either. If the profound joy of our deepest unity fills our hearts, we shall not be afraid of anyone. The reverence of perfect love drives out the fear of men. Whoever fears God fears no man. And perfect love drives out fear.

PRESENT EXPERIENCE —
FUTURE KINGDOM

T HE WORK OF JESUS grew out of the
activity of John the Baptist. John's proclamation
was the prophetic message of the future State
of social justice, of God's kingdom which shall
come to this earth. Like all prophets, he too
wanted to pave the way for the new hoped-for
conditions by transforming hearts and deeds.
His call to repentance demanded complete
revolution of the inner and outer life. He wanted
to remove the obstacles of personal and social
wrong which keep the individual away from
God's kingdom. He had to insist on complete
transformation, because he felt that God's kingdom was near. What mattered to him was the
real fruits, the right results of repentance. What
he demanded was a simple, plain morality.
Whenever people asked him what they should

do now he expressed point blank the absolute nature of surrender as the only way to social justice. If someone has two coats, let him share with him who has none; and if he has food, let him do likewise.

But when whole crowds of people came to his baptism to find forgiveness and renewal, John felt that another had to bring the Spirit, the transforming, sanctifying Spirit, without which the new conditions cannot take root. This other one was the longed-for Messiah, the just, peacemaking King of God's kingdom. Therefore the greatest event in the Baptist's life was the recognition that this longed-for Messiah had appeared — in Jesus.

Jesus took up John's message literally. Whoever does not doubt that John is concerned with the future State of God *on earth* cannot dispute it in Jesus either. He too was directed by the closeness of God's kingdom. Everything He had to say was very closely related to the revolution in earthly conditions which He expected from God.

But Jesus baptized in Spirit indeed. If we let His words work on us directly we are gripped by a refreshing wind which penetrates all our pores. He brings a new domain of life, a strength and a joy never known to us before. This is why Jesus, when a friend of the Baptist's movement asked an unspoken question concerning God's kingdom, answered, "What is born of the flesh is flesh, and what is born of the Spirit is spirit," "Anyone who is not born of water and the Spirit cannot enter the kingdom of God." Jesus declares that it is impossible to gain the right vision for the future kingdom without such a new birth. In this, as in all other things, he lives in the prophetic truth which knows that law and society can be transformed only through religious and moral renewal of the spiritual life.

Jesus told us much more clearly and much more deeply than all the prophets what the characteristic traits of this Spirit are, without which we can gain neither inner renewal nor the earthly future State. In the Sermon on the Mount He gives in detail the inner substance, the program of His proclamation, "Repent, for the kingdom is at hand."

We all know the Beatitudes blessing the poor, the suffering, the merciful, and the loving, who shall possess the kingdom of heaven. Yet how few people consider what shape this earthly kingdom is to take in accordance with the will of the preacher on the mount. How seldom do people see the moral demands implied when only those are called blessed who give their lives solely to acting for peace and longing for justice. Are there more than a handful of people who realize the ethical implications of this?

We realize that the absolute will for peace, the absolute justice of love cannot be demanded by any moral law. Nobody will have the courage to lay such demands on himself or on others. Yet nobody was less moralistic and less legalistic than Jesus. The new justice — better than, and different from, moralism and coercion — shall penetrate the world like salt and light in free, spontaneous working. The light would become dark and the salt insipid if unconditional love were no longer to control our lives completely. God's kingdom is the kingdom of love in the pure sense of the word. Its ethic knows of no exceptions or qualifications, because love is free life-energy and cannot be held back.

The Spirit of God's kingdom brings about such a liberation from all murderous impulses and actions that men who are gripped by it cannot injure anyone's human dignity or live unreconciled with anyone. This perfect love and respect for men means faithfulness, above all in engagement and marriage. This love knows no weapons but its own: to meet others all the way and joyfully to dedicate oneself. That is why this love lets itself be struck on both cheeks; it gives away the overcoat too when somebody claims the jacket. This love is a love to neighbor and enemy alike, it is a love of unrestricted helpfulness, it is the will to bless unconditionally. This love is the airstream into which Jesus immerses His friends completely, so that they no longer live in any other sphere. This spirit of love is a fresh wind of truthfulness, honesty and genuineness, of simpleness and uprightness. It has no part in the sultry atmosphere of unhealthy emotionalism and pathological self-reflection. That is why Jesus hates the sensational and seeks to be unobtrusive in all His actions. He loves to be simple, concise and brief in His communing with God and in His dealings with people.

We can now see the deep differences which can open up between man and man and in the life of the individual. Jesus feels that His divine Spirit of love stands in sharpest opposition to the spirit of Mammon and its will to power. He expresses this as a sharp alternative. Do not lay up treasures on earth for yourselves. You cannot serve God and Mammon. Only the inner firmness and resolve of the heart for God, only the self-discipline of the soul for its highest goal, liberates us from self-seeking, from vassalage of every kind. Only if the justice of the divine State of the future is our first and our last longing are we truly free, free from worry, free from our degenerate, self-centered life.

To experience this justice means to be flooded by love. It creates such a fine feeling for the inner and outer necessities of our fellowmen that we must do the same good to them which we would like to receive from them. Whatever you wish that men would do to you, do the same to them.

This short talk by Jesus, though generally known to Christians as the Sermon on the Mount, has remained completely unrecognized by them. It is a sweeping outline of the characteristics of that inner life which alone can give rise to a true social life among men — the life of God's future State. The secret of this talk is the secret of God's kingdom, and as such it can be revealed only in God himself. The future kingdom can only be hoped for, expected, seized and taken hold of as communion in God, as organic union with Him. The prayer in this talk is therefore the Lord's Prayer.

It is incomprehensible dishonesty in the human heart to pray daily that this kingdom should come, that God's will should be done on earth as in heaven, and at the same time to try to deny that Jesus wanted this kingdom and the ethic it demands of men to be put into practice on the earth. Whoever asks for the absolute rulership of God to come down on earth believes in this will and is wholeheartedly resolved to carry it out. But anyone who emphasizes that the Sermon on the Mount is impractical and weakens its moral obligations should be mindful of its concluding words, "Not all who say to me 'Lord,' shall reach the kingdom of heaven, but only those who do the will of my Father in heaven."

But there are many who think that in His parables of the kingdom Jesus warped the message of the Sermon on the Mount in such a way that later He no longer spoke of a future

State, but only of a present sphere of influence of God's kingdom. But to try to place these two things in opposition to each other is to misjudge the crucial content of Jesus' experience. These people try to reconcile the supposed contradictions of the parables in such a way that the absolute character of the future stands opposed to God's working in the present, which they consider to be relative, weakened and adapted. Jesus, however, speaks in parables because only these paradoxical pictures are able to contain and convey the absolute as the basic experience of God's kingdom.

The kingdom of God is absolute. Its love is unconditional. Its social justice is perfect. Its ethic is direct and straightforward. We are surrounded everywhere by the relative, the imperfect, the conditonal, and by that which accommodates itself to circumstances. Whoever lives, like Jesus, utterly in the absolute, unconditional and perfect, possesses God and His kingdom in the present. That is why Jesus had to testify about himself that in His person the kingdom of God had arrived among men. Because His experience of the absolute was unfeigned, His life was free of the relativities of His environment. What He was in himself, and what He possessed, had a forming and transforming effect on His environment.

That is why the reports of healings of the sick essentially belong to the picture of Jesus. Therefore, when He sent out His messengers He made these things a necessary condition for the genuineness of their message that the kingdom of God is at hand: healing of the sick and raising of the dead, also having the simplest gear to the point of being penniless.

Faith in the absoluteness of God's will for the present is identical with the expectation of His kingdom. The same intensity of inner experience belongs to both. The two are interdependent to such a degree that the future expectation of perfect justice is given through the present attitude of absolute love, and vice versa. However, as in all genuine experiences of the eternal, this can never be a matter of defining the future in terms of computable periods of time. What the Spirit brings about is a reaching across all spaces, a "being one" in the Spirit with the God-given future which leaves no feeling of distance in time whatever.

Like scattered seed, this experience brings

forth, quite spontaneously, the corresponding attitude of perfect love. The restricting force of care and of wealth, anti-divine Mammon as the real enemy of spontaneous life, can choke it only if the will is open to this hostile influence. Since this is a matter of the most subtle spiritual process, particularly in its initial stages, it is impossible to determine in every instance where the absolute Spirit is quietly unfolding its influence. Useless and good plants must grow together until the harvest.

Like every organic growth, the kingdom of God begins as in a single seed. Yet the more it unfolds its life the more joy and help it is able to give. The life of the Jesus-man is a life of unreserved love and devotion, of single-hearted work for peace and will for social justice; it influences the great world as leaven works in a lump of dough. Yet leaven can only do this if it remains unadulterated and keeps its full strength. For the new life is like a precious pearl, a buried treasure of immense value, to be won only by those who give up everything else for it.

Only this absolute Spirit of the Sermon on the Mount makes it possible to experience the kingdom of God. In the parable of the entrusted funds the unity between present experience and the future State is shown most clearly. He who has been at work and has been doing things in this world with the powers of the divine Spirit entrusted to him, without hiding or concealing them, shall be put in charge of broad areas of country and city in the future State.

The kingdom of God cannot be of the world as it is today. Yet it is *for* the world, in order to exercise the strongest effect on it, and, in the end, to transform it completely. The Jesus-people are sent out to work among men, to be effective in the world, just as Jesus himself was sent into the world. That is why their task and their actions cannot be different from His own: to bring help and deliverance for soul and body, for the life of the spirit and for economic life. Like Jesus they have to represent the message of the future kingdom, to heal and to help in all men's sufferings and torments.

Like Jesus, His people too have to overcome the temptation to produce bread by devilish means or to conquer political realms in contradiction to God's Spirit. They have been sent like defenseless sheep among murderous wolves, and they have nothing to do with their ways of fighting. Only the Spirit, only love, is their weapon. In obedience to the word of their Lord they have sheathed their swords. Yet they feel that the Spirit which was in Jesus is the mightiest power, which no other power can resist. They do not want to forget to which Spirit they belong as children. Since He who sent them does not want to destroy life but only to save life, they cannot send destructive fire on people and on cities. The only fire Jesus kindled is the fire of love. There was nothing He wanted more than that this warming light and fire should be spread over the whole earth.

But Jesus knew what kind of resistance had to be overcome before the victory could be won in the realm of the Spirit, without which nothing can be won in the lower regions — government and economics. The absolute can only be won by totality. The life of God will only be won by complete firmness of will. This is why the old, degenerate life must be abhorred to gain the new, genuine life. One must hate father and mother, wife and child and in all things hate one's own life wherever it wants to disturb and destroy the new life.

This is why Jesus advises the young man who had become very dear to Him to sell all his possessions, to follow Him, and to live for the poor. This is why He himself did not even own a place to sleep, and why He said to His friends, "Sell what you have and do justice .... Whoever does not renounce all that he has cannot be my disciple."

To regard this as a negation of the earthly is to misjudge the real and essential. Jesus emphasizes that ownership or abundance of earthly goods can never be life or give life. He impresses it upon us that to be able to find true happiness on earth and in life we must beware of love of money in every form. He puts the gathering of treasures in opposition to being rich in God. Gathering in the richest harvest and erecting large, new buildings cannot benefit us if we lose our life. God gives us each day we are allowed to live. God fills it with its rich content of love when we learn to acquire the riches of God.

Money, which Jesus calls unjust Mammon in this context, has only one advantage: to make friends through the love which shares and gives away, and to win that love which can never perish. For love must bring forth love. It is the only wealth of life; it alone can make life fully alive. This is why only that man who has surrendered and overcome his selfishness really gains his life. Therefore Jesus calls complete love to God the greatest love in a man's life. He sees it wherever we love our fellowmen as much as we love ourselves. He who does not have this love lacks the most important thing, the only thing which is truly alive, however much piety he may show. He lacks the sense for justice; he lacks mercy and faithfulness.

Whoever lives in this Spirit draws the kingdom of God into the present. Where this Spirit is alive as in Jesus, the kingdom of God rushes in violently and is won by storm. It reveals itself everywhere as the good news for the poor, as the liberation of the oppressed and enslaved, of the imprisoned and the crushed. It reveals that class antagonisms in society are overcome to such a degree that the poor and the incapacitated are invited instead of the rich and the relatives, that the strongest love and justice is bestowed on social outcasts. Just as Jesus has the strongest compassion for the sick and the sinners, so also those who have His Spirit feel drawn in their deepest heart to those who seem to be the victims of discrimination and prejudice in every respect, because of their own guilt or that of others. He who experiences this justice of love will never feel like a benefactor distributing his alms condescendingly, but like a man who recognizes for himself and for his fellow men the same calling to be true men.

Of such people Jesus says that they are not conscious of the charitable and Christly character of their lives. They live for the hungry and the thirsty, for the homeless and naked, for the sick and for the imprisoned. Yet they do not know what they have done until they are told, "Whatever you have done to one of these, the least of my brothers, you have done to me." A Jesus life of this kind is steeped so deeply in the spirit of brotherliness that in it nobody strives for a high position, but only for the simplest way of serving and helping. And this service is for all men. Whoever lies by the roadside and whoever is in any kind of need is my neighbor, and to him I am allowed to give my love.

In a special way the enemy is this one. He is a neighbor who either has suffered because of me and mine, or who draws the greatest harm to himself because of his hostility. A special love belongs to him. His resistance can be overcome only by a stream of genuine, cordial affection, by real acts of good intention and of practical service, by honest intercession for the adversary. That is why antagonism should be overcome in its beginnings by obliging the enemy in every way possible and offering him every possible settlement before it has come to a real state of war or a lawsuit.

A life of this nature is only possible if we can become young, spontaneous and trusting, again and again. Only a life born out of unconstrained feeling, out of childlike, genuine emotion, which wants to love all people the way children do, can be capable of such an attitude. We can become one with God only through this same childlike trust; because of this Jesus said, "Whoever does not receive the kingdom of God like a child cannot enter." The kingdom of God belongs to the young, to the childlike.

Youth is stormy. Young people love the absolute and the true, the genuine and the spontaneous. This is why young people are those revolutionaries of whom Jesus says that they seize the Kingdom as if by violence. Since Jesus came, the kingdom of God rushes in with force wherever it is taken by force.

It is the same as with a man who is buried alive in a cave-in. In the lethally compressed and foul air he suddenly clutches open a gap so as to allow the free fresh airstream to rush in. In such a moment the one thus liberated feels completely united with the other world he longs for, even though he cannot yet step out into it. In the same way we who are in the prison of the present moment are overwhelmed by the powers of eternity as soon as we dare to draw in the eternal and the absolute, the divine and the perfect toward ourselves.

JOYFUL NEWS OF THE KINGDOM

WHEN WE FEEL TOO WEAK to do the task set us, what we lack is the love of Christ, the love that is poured into our hearts by the Holy Spirit. This love has none of the unclarity of human thinking, human feeling. There is nothing unclear in the direction of its will.

The love of Jesus is revealed in His life in perfect clarity. The power of Jesus' life, sealed by the Holy Spirit in His death and resurrection, was poured out upon the first church in Jerusalem. This is the Spirit of whom it was foretold that He would recall the words of Jesus and throw clear light on His life; that He would reveal the future and would convict the world of sin, in righteousness and judgment. Sin was revealed as unbelief in Jesus. Righteousness was revealed by the Holy Spirit through the fact that Jesus has occupied the throne of God and brings the dominion of the eternal kingdom. Judgment was revealed through the prince of this world being judged by the love of Jesus Christ. This prince is the spirit of the times who controls all peoples, the spirit of might who is named a liar and murderer from the beginning. He was judged by the love of Jesus Christ, not by a forcible, violent deed of God's Son, but by the revelation of Jesus in His living and dying as the best, the most loving One.

Whoever takes His side is free from the earth spirit that is judged. Whoever wants to follow the latter yields to falsity, lying, and unfaithfulness, and is judged along with the earth spirit. Whoever wants to follow Jesus does not accept destruction, the works of the devil.

Wherever the church of Jesus truly is, there the Holy Spirit reigns as the revelation of Jesus Christ and discloses what the future of Jesus means. All this and more has been revealed through the outpouring of the Spirit. Yet this is already clear through all that was in Jesus' life. What Jesus did, like what He said, revealed perfect love. First of all it is evident that Jesus is perfect love for God. Out of this love everything He did was born. Because of this He received the baptism of John, consecrating himself to death, and after this He cried out, "The kingdom of God is at hand."

Even before this, His love for God was victorious in the threefold temptation. The tempter, the spirit of the earth, the prince of the world, had challenged him to take possession of all the world's thrones by allying himself with the spirit of lying and impurity. The same tempter challenged Him to proclaim His own greatness by manifesting His own tremendous supremacy over the laws of nature; he wanted Him to show that He was God's Son by prevailing over the law of gravity in the presence of all the people. And he wanted to give Him a large amount of bread for the people, to use as a weapon to make himself popular.

But Jesus loved God, His Father, above all. He drove Satan off and lived God's kingdom, not by ruling the kingdom, not by winning mankind over as such, but alone by the power of His love for God. Be gone, Satan! You shall serve God alone. Man does not live by bread alone, but by every inflaming word from God's loving heart.

This is the word He was to proclaim. *God* is what is at stake. He alone must rule: Prepare yourselves for this. Human history shows mighty events, but none of them comes anywhere near the coming of God. When God's kingdom comes — that alone will be real history; then something will really happen.

Here is the crucial thing: Love Him. Change yourselves and your lives. Everything must tumble. Change your thinking. Believe the joyful news that God is near. Repent. Believe in the joyful news.

Jesus not only proclaimed this good news through parables. He also stated its meaning in clear, unmistakable words: God is coming; His rulership is approaching. The Gospel of John, in reporting about Nicodemus, says that man must be renewed in such a way that he begins all over again like a baby; he must be newborn. A completely new beginning has to be made. New birth has meaning only in the sense of being born anew for God's kingdom. It cannot be entered without new birth. God's kingdom — this alone is what counts.

The nature of the new beginning is portrayed in Matthew's Gospel. The Sermon on the

Mount shows how the new life of rebirth brings a righteousness, a goodness, that is incomparably better than any morals, any theology, anything that has ever been said or thought. This new righteousness is God's doing; it is the outpouring of His Spirit, the true being of the light that is to come, the saltiness of salt. It is essence and power, most vivid aliveness, freedom in movement. This new righteousness is life born of God. Man must be beggar-poor before he can find it. He must first take the world's suffering upon himself. He must desire peace in a peaceless world. He must long for goodness and love. He must be ready for sacrifice, even death. Then he will know and experience God's heart, he will find God himself, if he is willing to suffer death for His justice and His kingdom.

Here the knowledge of God's kingdom begins. Here enemies are loved; one's last penny is given away out of love; force is not repaid with force. Here is fidelity and purity. This is the better righteousness; here the better, the complete love is revealed, and everlasting faithfulness in love.

You in your way should be perfect, like the Father. There is no perfection other than that of love. So be aware of the things that thwart this love: property and worry! Wherever possessions are heaped up while fellow human beings go hungry and cold, there is no love. Therefore gather no wealth for yourselves. A worrier is building his life on wealth just as much as a wealthy man. Away with this! Do not worry. Look at the birds and flowers. Do believe in the loving God, the Father, who provides everything.

What you need is an undivided heart; your eye must concentrate on God only. The heart is like an inward eye; it must focus upon its object. In your hearts your view must be undivided and concentrated; it must be solely for God. Then you will have no wealth and no worry. You can then grasp that to call upon God in prayer is to trust in His love; it is to implore His rulership, the doing of His will, the honoring of His name. Thus it is your daily bread. This is how you shall be freed from evil and temptation. This is how you must call to God.

Do not judge men; love them. But you must not reveal what is holiest in your hearts to people who are not ready for it. But do not judge them either; for that would be sinning against love for God and men. God's love is greater than your condemnation. Only God knows the heart of the guilty one in its depths. Treat him as you yourselves would wish to be treated. You would want God to provide for you. All those things that you expect for yourselves, do for all men and give to all men, without exception. You should not set limits to the good deeds you do out of love. After all, God loves human beings, no matter what they are like.

Truth expressed in loving deed — this is the narrow gate, the entry into God's kingdom; it is the only true reality in your lives. Love people just as you love yourselves, because you love God. You take care of yourselves in body, soul, and spirit. You should do exactly the same for others; only then will you know the gate to the kingdom of God.

Even if there are only very few of you, still, go this way. Disturbing spirits and powers will turn up. Know the false prophets by their acts, their predatory nature. The true prophet can be recognized by the love he has — the love that gives up his own life for his beloved brothers. Know him by the lamb's nature.

Jesus disclosed the character of this new way of life, of this new structure, that cannot be toppled. This was how He proclaimed the truth everywhere.

It was not long before the hostility to Jesus grew severe. The guile and cunning His opponents used to entrap Him by theological argument made Him decide, after sending out the apostles, to restrict himself to parables. These were meant to veil the truth from the meddlesome and impudent who wanted to listen only so as to confute. To hearts that were open He disclosed the entire mystery of the kingdom of God. The ultimate meaning of His message of God's kingdom is revealed in the parables of the wedding and the banquet, symbols of the fellowship of many in sharing what is entrusted to them by God. Thus the kingdom of heaven is compared to the wedding and the banquet feast.

God's kingdom consists in doing. Hence it is compared to the workers in the vineyard. The point is to *do yes* even though one may say no. What matters is the seed that must be sown so that it can multiply, blessed by heaven. It depends on the sower. Only through uttermost preparedness can the kingdom of love, unity and work be attained.

The new substance of the new kingdom cannot be patched onto the old garment of the old kingdom. Everything must be given away for the priceless jewel, the kingdom of God. The only path to God's kingdom is to sell all and leave all behind.

This kingdom of God is at first like a ferment or leaven in bread dough, worked into the entire substance of human life. It is like a grain of seed. But it grows, and in growing its significance becomes that of a tree beneath which everything can live. Even though the enemy may scatter among the good seed his counterfeit weeds, do not use force. Both must be left to grow until the harvest.

The character of the comrades of this kingdom must be like the kingdom itself — strong like a rock or a tree; fruitful like a fruit-b ng tree. Their nature is the love and joy shown in the banquet and the wedding garment. Their character is the inward readiness that we see in the parable of the virgins. This character must be tenacious, persistent in patience; it must be faithful and vigilant, like the loyal steward and servant in the parable. It is active persevering love; and this is not present where one indulges in one's own pleasure, as in the parable of the rich man.

This character is first and foremost that of a humble heart, free of all self-importance; it is that of the man in the temple who cried out, "God, have mercy on me, sinner that I am!" The character of the comrades of the kingdom is the heart that goes to look for the strayed sheep, that accepts the prodigal son back into the household, that seeks to bring men into fellowship with God before the door is closed. Here is the true flock, the true fold, the true Shepherd, the true pasture. Here is real community. Love for the individual and for the whole — this is love to God. The entire mystery can be compared to a plantation: organic unity is like a grapevine. Individuals are the branches; the whole grapevine is Christ himself and His Holy Spirit.

Once again Christ finally summed up His truth, in sharp opposition to false prophecy. His love rejects evil to the utmost and combats it. He cries out the sevenfold "Woe!" and proclaims the catastrophe of God's judgment upon all who betray and forsake Him. It is because of these words that He was executed as an enemy of men, an enemy of the best state and the best church.

Jesus carried out in deeds everything that He said. His life was the *doing* of love, above all in gathering His twelve and His seventy and sending them out. He showed that He was able to carry the burden of fellowship, that He was capable of living in community, by the way He "stuck it out" with them in a life of complete sharing, also in the way He taught His disciples as His pupils. The Gospels are written out of this daily teaching of Jesus, in which He told and explained everything in many different ways. As is said at the end of the Gospel of John, Jesus did many more things, but if they were all written down the world would not hold the books that would have to be written.

The things Jesus did while among His disciples and companions proved His love by what He did to body, soul, and spirit, according to their degree of readiness. It was His *actions* that demonstrated what it will be like when God's kingdom comes. The driving out of demons, the rule of God's kingdom, the healing

of sickness — all these are part and parcel of
the conquest of the death spirit. Jesus healed
people of leprosy and skin diseases. He healed
the blind, cured women of their sickness, healed
the lame and the man with the withered arm.
He took away fever, made the deaf-mute speak
and hear; He straightened the deformed woman, awakened from death bodies already in
corruption. Those He raised from death were
Lazarus, the young man at Nain, and the little
daughter of Jairus.

Along with all this, by mastering the elements
Jesus showed what His way was of proving
God's love. He fed the four thousand and the
five thousand, He calmed the storm, and transformed water into wine, as a sign of His love,
of His participation in joy.

By these many things that Jesus did He
showed that outward healing is the symbol and
sign of something greater, something crucial. It
is a demonstration of how the love of God at the
end of the days will do everything which belongs
to love for the bodies of men also. Matter is not
excluded from God's kingdom and His rule.

But God's love turns at the same time towards
the inward life, so as to prepare the soul for

God's kingdom. Go, and do evil no more! By healing both outwardly and inwardly, Jesus manifested His authority to forgive. Forgiveness is healing; it is removal; evil and sickness are gone. Healing is the symbol of forgiveness; it is the sign that when Jesus comes the force of the evil one is removed. This is why the resurrection from the dead had to happen. God had to be demonstrated as unconquerable life. Death is the last enemy and must be defeated if God is to rule.

God is life because God is love. God is love because He is life. As such He is resurrection. Thus it is that Jesus arose from the dead and was revealed as the Living One. He is present in the outpouring of the Holy Spirit. The experience of the Spirit's outpouring is the fulfilling of the words, "I am with you all the days." The King of the kingdom is the Spirit; the King of God's kingdom and the Spirit of the church are one. Jesus is present in His whole authority wherever the Holy Spirit of love is at work. This is the certainty of the gospel.

GOD AND THE FUTURE OF MEN

WE ARE NOT YET MEN; this is not yet humanity. But in us lives the demand and the promise that we must become men and that humanity shall be. This demand is absolute. It cannot be twisted. It cannot be weakened. It cannot be relativized into something conditional. It cannot be adapted to just any circumstances. It cannot be changed. It remains what it is: the demand to become men, the demand for humanity to be united, the demand and the promise that is contained in this demand, the certainty that burns through us from this demand. It is direct. It cannot be conveyed to us through men; it cannot be passed on through lectures or meetings. It cannot be forced on us by even the mightiest powers. It cannot be transmitted to us by any priest. It tolerates no intermediaries.

This certainty is direct and spontaneous. It lives in men's hearts. It is the conscience of all men. The conscience is the most certain of all certainties. The conscience of the individual is one with the conscience of the whole. The conscience of the whole tends toward the solidarity of all men in all things, toward the future fellowship of all in the peace and justice of the coming time. Even the best that we find today in relationships between us modern men is weak. At best it is but a suggestion, a parable of the good which we all want. Even the best human being we meet is but a weakened and broken allusion to that which alone is important, that for which he is destined to live.

Mankind is a prism; or rather, it is less than that. Each human being is but an invisibly small line in the endlessly evolving spectrum of humanity into which God's sunlight breaks up. In Christ this light appeared once in its clear, white brightness and purity. In Him are contained all colors in the endless play of colors of being and becoming human — all except for the bad. The light of man's calling comes from

God, just as the sun is the original white light of the solar spectrum contained in the colors of the rainbow.

The light is God. The growing church community of the coming era is the prism in its entirety; it is a spectrum with the play of all colors. Each believing individual in it is only one infinitely small, fine line in this band of color, only a hint, a weakened form in one single hue. But only in the totality of all the infinite number of colors, in the combining of all colors gathered up into the entire prism of the future, will the bright, pure, one light of the sun again become clear and all-inclusive. Everything else — that which exists today — is mutual service as diverse as the many different colors. And the crowning of this mutual service is harmony, the unity of the many contrasting lights in whiteness, the uniting of all colors in pure, clear white.

Harmony is the wholeness of the many; it is unity in variety, richness in diversity. Here is the secret of life: that we are called to this harmony of sounds, to this harmony of colors. That this world becomes harmony is the goal of life. Whatever we stammer about the organism of the human body, the astronomic rhythm of the heavens and the development of mankind's history, is neither more nor less than a glimmering, an intimation of this unknown harmony, a guidepost pointing to the real, the significant, which is infinitely more than, and utterly different from, all the rest.

A picture never is the object that it represents. But it shows the object of which it is a likeness. So too, the parable of the coming era, the future toward which we are moving in history, is not this final thing. What we shall experience in the coming things of mankind's coming unity, the common work that will be, is not the eternal, endless perfection; it is not the completion. And yet it is the highest that can befall human history. It is the parable of what is eternal in the world history of mankind, the parable of the times. That which is to come over the earth as the new time, that which we see coming with immediate certainty and which we feel is directed to us, absolutely and inexorably, as the religious and moral demand of the moment, is a decisive parable of the eternal and infinite will which embraces mankind and world history, a parable of the harmony of all heavenly spheres and all epochs.

Our words about "God" are nothing but

weak human stammering. The charges constantly made against the word "God" have a certain justification. To say that the name of "God," when we pronounce it, is utter blasphemy has a deep, divine justification. For what we say about God, what we think about God, what we address as divine, the way we abuse the name of God in our preaching — all that is downright blasphemy. The very claim or presumption to speak of God, which I too have taken upon myself here as destiny and guilt — this very claim and presumption is an enormous burden for man's weak shoulders. It is clear that all we utter about God is not God. Whatever we speak about God comes no closer to Him than the dust on our streets can come to the furthest star.

And yet when we are gripped by the God whom we cannot express or think, when we are seized by the majesty of His actual existence, by the tremendous might of His coming, by His intervention in temporal history and the physical world, then we cannot be silent. Woe to us if we withhold the tidings about Him!

In mankind's history the tidings of God have emerged over and over again. This religious history of the concepts and proclamations of God must not be confused with God himself either. We must not think that this development of words about God and feelings men have had about God are the same as that which only God himself can be. He is the Unchangeable. "I am who I am" is His name. The concepts we have of Him, the thoughts we entertain about Him, the feelings impressed on us by Him change and pass, but God remains. It is not God who is in question. There is no question about God. But everything we say and think about this God, everything we confess to feeling God to be, all this is what is questionable; here is where the question mark belongs.

Nevertheless, in the stammering of this age-old human history and religious history going back thousands of years, God himself is at work. Man can only speak in metaphors or parables. The deepest spokesmen of the eternal and endless truth spoke in images; not, of course, images invented by themselves, but images of reality in heaven and earth. Only in these symbolic parables of living reality can the divine be sensed. The only way faith can express itself is by vision and action. There is no faith that does not give birth to a visual concept of life and the world. There is no faith that does not give growth to deed. Vision and deed are the language of faith. Whatever we utter in sermon, book and lecture about the things of faith has strength and life only in so far as the vision of true life and the deed of true life are alive and present in what we say. There is nothing more degraded and hellish than the preaching of hollow words that have neither the vision of reality nor action in real life behind them.

Mankind's history is the history of the intuitive awareness of last things. It is the history of God's testimony in the vision of reality and in the doing of His will. We recognize God only by doing His will. We cannot recognize God by reading books, by higher education or other ways of trying to approach His mystery through reflection or through our feelings. God can be recognized only by becoming one with Him, in deed and in truth.

Between beings of spirit there is only one mutual recognition, that of becoming one with one another. Outwardly we can recognize physical things, not filled with spirit, that we encounter. Beings with spirit cannot be recognized outwardly, from a distance and without participation. We cannot get to know a single human being if we remain strange and distant and hostile to him. As long as mistrust and rejection remain between us like a physical wall, it is impossible to recognize the essential being of a fellow man. Not until the moment we become one with the innermost spirit, the innermost will of our brother human being, not until that moment will we know him.

No beings of spirit can be known by us unless we unite with what is best in them by surrendering our will. The history of man's intuitions about God is a history of this knowing-through-uniting, this trembling, hesitating, growing recognition ever in peril of being lost.

In primitive men, men of the ice age and the stone age, we see that in gathering around the burning, flickering, flashing, warming fire and in the funeral rites and burial of their loved ones they had a presentiment of faith in God; we see that surrender and sacrifice to this spirit of the universe was the essence of reverence for God from the very beginning.

Mana, says the primitive African or Hottentot

of the objects and natural phenomena in which he feels a power, a force that is superior to himself. Mana, the superior might of an inexplicable force in all things. Mana, the mystery of the sky and its constellations, the mystery of fire and of flowing water; mana, the secret of thunder and lightning; mana, the secret of magnetism and of mutual physical attraction; mana, the mystery of birth, the secret of all secrets. This is the collective name, the allusion by which uncivilized peoples show their reverence and longing for God's power.

Totem, they call the animals in which this mysterious all-pervading universal power appears as the particular capacity for unity and for mutual service which we call social instinct. The most primitive peoples are communistic peoples; they are men who live in fellowship of goods, working tools and materials, of land and the tilling of fields. The power called mana, this mysterious might of the living God in all things, is most strongly revealed to them through the image of the social instinct in the animal world. Totem is the word by which primitive man signifies that the social instinct is alive in the animal world.

Tabu, says the savage, and is afraid. Icy shudders trickle down his back when he senses God's power in those natural forces and social instincts, when he sees them in wild animals and all the stormy elements. Tabu means reverence, trembling; it means that the human heart bows before superior force, that the heart bows, keeps its distance, and becomes small, in the face of powers that we men are not able to control, powers that overwhelm us. Anyone who has some understanding for what is simple feels how the intuitive awareness of God that flashes up in this childlike, original, savage type of man is the same as that found on the highest religious level of concepts of God in theologized expressions.

The real, critical danger to religious life that we meet in the highest theology, in the most highly developed church and sect, is just the same as what we find in primitive people too, primitive Africans and Hottentots, and in the ice age peoples. The *fetish* is the idolizing of God's power in things; the fetish is idolization of holy animals, idolization of that reverence and trembling, in some object. It makes no difference whether this object is carried about like the host in a golden vessel, or whether it is thought to be built up or built in with holy walls in a holy building; whether this object is supposed to be hidden in a grove outside in nature on a mountain, in some animal or in the magic power of magnetic suggestion by some priest. It makes no difference whether certain other things are thought to represent this power and might of God, such as pictures or crucifixes, rosaries or amulets, or images of idols in the most primitive form. It makes no difference whether it is communism or hierarchy, orthodoxy or sectarianism; whether it is an altar, a table or a bench, a book or an instrument.

The idolizing of religious life by materializing objects, as in mammonism, in money, proves to be the prime danger of the religious life. And as soon as this idolization has set in, as soon as this one object, this one thing or certain number of things has taken the place of the all-embracing God, of the one Spirit at work in all who want to live and believe, then the God that people still talk about has in fact become the devil.

In the Babylonians, the first civilization that we encounter in the history of our globe, we find this enormous tension between the true God of the all-inclusive spirit of fellowship and that devilish spirit of idolization carried to sinister extremes. We read in our Bible, in the Psalms, about Jehovah, the Lord of hosts who rules over the spirits and holds the stars in His hands, who sends forth the spirits that inhabit these stars as His messengers, His angels, His servants, ministering spirits. This faith in the God who rules in the astronomic heaven and who will also rule over this earth, this faith in the highest God in the world of stars is the faith of the Babylonians too. The highest God is the God of heaven. He is ruler of the star worlds.

On this earth God does not reign yet as He rules in the heavens. This earth is subject to sinister powers. Fearful hosts of demons with the most violent and darkest might are passing through the nations and over the earth. Again and again night broods over our planet. But ever again the stars break through the darkness of this night. And the God of heaven, who has His seat in the heights of the northern sky, who reigns there in the remotest constellations, is attacked again and again by the upward-threatening darkness of the blue-black night of heaven in the sign of the dragon; but in every one of these oppressive nights the radiant planets rise, led by Venus and Mars.

These brilliant wandering bodies travel the light-path of the zodiac; they hurry through the sky with flaming torches, thus proving constantly anew the victory of light over darkness as a holy symbol, a marvelous representation of the light-victory of the eternal and living God who rules in the heavens. The moon rises with them and races through the same course. Its own existence offers the same symbolic representation of the coming of light that is shown by the heavenly courses of the planets. Out of the ashes of its darkness at the time of the new moon it arises again and again as the waxing moon, until as the full moon it triumphs over the darkness.

A still more powerful sign of victorious light is the sun. When the night is at its deepest and coldest, the morning star precedes the sun, and the sun appears—the victory of God's eternal light over the darkness. Thus in every night watch, every morning of a new day, certainty is strengthened for the Babylonians that the God who lives in the heavens will also enter upon His reign of light on the earth.

We all know the story of the three wise men from the Orient. This story is doubtless historical. It contains the secret of the entire Babylonian culture. Those three men from the Babylonian East had seen a star in the heavens. At a quite definite place in the sky a new star had flashed up out of the darkness, a star of unprecedented whiteness and brightness, the sudden phenomenon of a new birth in the star world.

From age-old libraries perhaps 5000 to 6000 years old we have exact knowledge today of the wisdom of the Babylonians. Tablets of clay and brick, each 1½ to 2 centimeters thick, make up a book series, each book containing 100 to 120 of these tablets. Thousands of such books have been found near Nineveh. Scholars have been assiduously deciphering these books. We know today that Babylon's astrological research aimed to define and classify all the lands of the whole earth—geography, that is—in accordance with the position of the celestial constellations. Just as one can make a projection from the ceiling to the floor simply by imagining a vertical line from each point on the ceiling to the floor, so that each point on the ceiling of the room corresponds to a point on the floor of the room, so too the scholars of that day strove to project each individual point in the astronomic heavens to a geographic point and so to apply astronomical events to the earth.

Those three wise men saw that unique star blaze up. In their age-old wisdom they were certain that the decisive Son of man was born who was to bring in the new time of love and unity. Already in that culture, as far back as 6000 years before our time, there was latent the certainty that one day, at the end of time, the kingdom of peace and justice must come over this earth; that the world of oneness and of the circle which according to Babylonian belief rules in the astronomical heavens shall one day be manifest on this earth too as unity and as the circle-relationship of true fellowship. The flashing up of that star at a very definite point in the astronomical sky meant for the learned men of that day the certainty that "he is born who alone is important for all the future." They projected this place in the sky onto the earth and declared: In Judea He must be born.

In the Egyptians, whose culture comes into the light of our historical investigation somewhat later than that of the Babylonians, we meet with a different aspect, a different expression of the same spirit, in regard to this geography, this division of the earth as illustrated by the constellations. While the Babylonians felt it was their task in the upper world to represent God's heavenly rulership for the earth, the Egyptians, people of the underworld, saw it as their task to proclaim the rulership of the same God for the human world of the dead.

The great Babylonian king wrapped a dark blue cloak about his limbs. This dark blue cloak of the heavens had embroidered upon it at carefully measured intervals all the silver-yellow constellations of the entire astronomical heavens. In this way the king of Babylon portrayed the task of representing in his person the majestic reign of God who was to come upon the earth. The king felt that he, in his heavenly cloak, dark blue as the night with its glistening stars, was called to represent this rulership of God on this earth, in the name of God and in the place of God.

Thus the great king of Babylon was at the same time the high priest of Babylonian religion. Priest and king, united in one person, exemplified the task and the demand that the unique power of the heavenly king be represented in one human being and brought to rulership on the earth. The king of Babylon believed that by the mighty edifices he erected, by the huge military campaigns he undertook, he was preparing the future lordship of the coming God upon this earth. The bigger his temple buildings were and the higher the Babylonian tower which he built as his temple-palace soared, the prouder he felt in his awareness of being a forerunner of the God who would come from heaven to conquer His earth for the world of stars.

The Babylonian tower, the tower of Babel, was nothing but a temple meant to represent the astronomic stratification of the world above. Below, the three layers of the earth were indicated in the structure of this temple, the atmosphere of our earth's air being the highest and outermost layer; then the earth's crust of rocks, soil and the water that floods it, as the ground beneath us; and under this the glowing lava of the earth's interior, as the bottomless depths of the sinister underworld.

Above this threefold stratification of the earth in the temple the courses of the seven planets were represented by the seven steps of a graded pyramid or *ziggurat*. Seven planets circled around the sun; seven signs of the revelation of light were seen in the astronomical heavens by the Babylonians. Just as the planets have their orbits in sevenfold removal from the sun, so seven great steps carried this Babylonian tower up to the heights. It was the task of this Babylonian king to build up, upon these seven steps, the endless height of the star world, gates reaching into heaven.

Here the starry heights of the rich Creator-God become just as vivid to us as man's titanic arrogance, his presumptuous religious pride. The human king steps into God's place. The man-made structure steps into the place of the creating God, in His star world and His earth.

While this was the form this took in the Babylonian world in the king's palace as the sign of the upper world of astronomic heavenly powers, in Egypt we find the reverse: the signs of the underworld. The Egyptian Pharaoh, too, felt that he was the representative of God in His great realm of the setting sun, just as all the little city-kings in the civilization of that time claimed to represent and manifest all-embracing

divine life. The Egyptian lands were bordered
on the west by the desert. The graves of the
Egyptians were placed out there in the hot
desert, where no embalming was necessary,
since bodies were preserved unchanged in the
burning heat and wind of the desert. So it was
the West that the Egyptian revered. Astrological
geography pointed out to him the decline, the
underworld, the realm of the dead toward
which sun, moon and planets descend.

Just as the East, the place where the light
rises, was the symbol of destiny in Babylon, so
in Egypt it was the West, the region of its setting. As in Babylon the tower strove to reach the
heights of the astronomical heavens, so in Egypt
the pyramid arose as the eternal monument of
the depths, the mighty grave of the Pharaohs.
Though dead and buried, they live enduringly,
having entered the underworld as lords of the
future who shall prove life's victory in the world
of day as well. Thousands of men worked for
decades on the job of preparing a huge grave
for one of these Pharaohs, a monument and
bulwark of amazing resistance, built of the hard-
est stones in a pointed pyramid that was meant
to defy for the longest time the storms and

tempests of the ages.

In the hidden chambers of these pyramids we find the temple of the Egyptians. Here the temple is a burial chamber, and in it is a simulated door through which the dead man goes in and out, as the living ruler of the world of the dead. In this burial chamber and the chambers around it, riches are provided for the dead man—whole herds of cattle, whole rooms full of clothing and food and conveniences, plenty of things and servants which he is supposed to need for an eternal life. And if objects, animals, and even people cannot be heaped up in sufficient quantity, their magical images are painted and burnt onto the walls. These images have a magical, sorcerous significance, because the artist has put the spell of life and power into these images.

To the right and left of these pyramids lie sphinxes to watch over them, desert jackals with human heads, demonic spiritual powers of living death in the form of half-beasts that are supposed to protect the pyramids from all injury and attack.

Behind all these concepts lies the conviction that the world of the dead too is ruled by God and that God is the life that triumphs over death. The legend of Osiris is the basic illustration for this belief. The king was murdered and his body was dismembered and thrown into the water, scattered at the mouth of the Nile. His wife, with their small child, looked for the dismembered corpse, found the pieces, fitted them together and laid them in a box or coffin. The dead man came alive and ruled as king of the underworld in the kingdom of the dead.

The Egyptians, then, are the people of belief in eternity for those who die; Egypt, with its belief in the destiny of everlasting life, is the land of human dignity. Yet in the Egyptians, too, whose certainty of resurrection is their foremost joy in the setting of the sun, even in the Egyptians, to whom the victory of light over death is revealed, the idolizing of faith in God makes its appearance most strongly.

There were Pharoahs in Tel-El-Amarna who translated their faith in the victory of light into the marvelous peace message of the one, sole God, contained in their Songs of the Sun. The sun's conquest of the darkness, the power of radiance and illumination of this radiant star without which we cannot live, was for them the

sign of the loving and peaceable nature and the
life power of the God who can be but One. All
these Pharaohs, however, who believed in the
victory of this Light-God, who out of the setting of the sun into the world of the dead saw
again and again the sun rising in the east as the
sign of resurrection for the dead—all these
Pharaohs believed this at bottom for themselves.
By rights, only the Egyptian Pharaoh, because
he was the priest-king, could actually be placed
on a level with Osiris, triumph over death
through faith in resurrection, attain the living
rulership in the underworld and be carried up
out of it into the astronomical heavens. Not
until the final epoch, when Egyptian religion
was completely transformed, did the claim arise
more and more strongly that each little human
being too in his modest grave must demand and
attain this belief in eternal life.

Here the power of the Middle and the North
had already broken in on the West, the power
which was to give the revelation to all men.
In the middle between the Egyptian and Babylonian civilizations lie Palestine and Arabia.
And from the east and the north the Medes
and the Persians threatened the Babylonian and

Salt and Light

Egyptian kingdoms. Mohammed and Zoroaster, the prophets of the Arabs and Persians, were recipients of a wealth of impressions from this sphere of Babylonian-Egyptian civilization, and they received words of truth and wisdom leading far beyond these impressions.

Zoroaster in his strong belief in the victory of light over darkness; Zoroaster who did not for a moment give himself up to any illusion about the fact that this earth lives in tremendous tension between good and evil; Zoroaster, who in spite of the seemingly evenly matched powers of light and darkness in the present world never lost the faith that still the light must have the total victory — he too saw in the course of the moon and the sun the symbolic astronomical portrayal of this victory of light. Zoroaster predicted, just for our present epoch of the current five hundred years, the great crucial turning point which we face today. To him the eternal voice sent out a call that stirred his inmost heart and hurled him forward into the surest vision of that which must come.

> "A voice in us is full of Holy Spirit.
> There is a thinking, a speaking and doing

as if you stood before God's presence.
There you have blest eternity,
and heaven and earth
lie at your feet.

Listen to this voice;
speak what it tells you to say;
do what it commands you,
and your thinking will be truth.
But know this:
truth's pulsing heart is God.

Yes, God, thou art the calling
of this voice,
thou within and without the same;
creating about me the earth,
beautifying it with fair meadows.
Thou askest only, Is it good?
and then thou givest it being.

This is what distinguishes the better man
from the evil man,
that he listens to this voice.
Here is the crossroads of the spirits;
here poverty, wealth and power
are nothing.

Help the good,
stamp out the bad.

For the voice, this voice of Holy Spirit,
does not lie.
And when it sees the evil around it,
it speaks a thunderous *no*.

For one day
it shall be a blazing flame,
where all reality becomes truth.
Then it will divide the better
from the bad;
it will consume in flames
and raise up in light.
Today it still gives kindly warning.
O hear!"

Mohammed, in the first period of his activity,
understood this prophetic vision of the future
in a similar way. Consciously following the
Jewish prophets and Jesus of Nazareth, and
strongly influenced at the same time by the
Babylonian and Egyptian religious cultures, he
set the task of energetically overcoming evil;
thus first he cultivated a withdrawal into isola-

tion and out of this asceticism inscribed on his banner the struggle for justice and for the earth. Like Zoroaster, Mohammed too made the demand that it should be men's particular task to apply truth and purity and justice to the distribution of land and work on the land. For half of his active time he lived in this type of prophetic proclamation. But then came the change. The power of sensuality, first in feelings of love for a nine-year-old girl, then for more and more girls and women, made him its captive. Temptation to bloody violence, ambition for great success, the demand for power by political conquest — which Jesus had rejected in His struggle with temptation — were the downfall of Mohammed. He became leader in an Arabian civil war, conquered Mecca and at the end of his life was preparing great military campaigns against Constantinople. His followers became the bloodhounds of Christianity, the men with the scimitar and the half moon, the waning moon, the upward-curved sickle. The idolization of religion, man's self-idolizing, confronts us here as in all other religious epochs, in Mohammed as an apostate prophet who defiled himself with futile filth and blood.

With such a man, it seems to us an oddity
buried in disordered chaos that his prophesying
of the last time in which the *Mahdi* is to come,
the Messiah, Jesus born of Mary, in whom
Mohammed believed as the future lord — that
this prophesying led to a belief by a Moham-
medan sect that saw the time from 1935 to 1950
as the most likely for the dawn of the new day.
Nevertheless it is not by coincidence that the
way leads us from these lands of the east and
the middle, from these two extrabiblical prophets, Zoroaster and Mohammed, into the most
familiar land of religious history, the land of
the Jews and Israelites.

The Bible we know. Mostly, however, we
do not recognize the Jewish and Israelite prophets as men who proclaimed the social revolution of all things, the conquest of the land and
the winning of the earth for the kingdom of
justice, for the prevalence of fellowship among
all men. It was clear to few that the prophets of
the Old Testament were the very men of mankind's history who prophesied most surely and
firmly a complete revolution of all things for
this earth, for our humanity on this earth. In
religious instruction it is usually taught only as

a deviation, a highly regrettable deviation of Jewish superstition, to apply God's kingdom to the life of the people, to the nations and earthly things; as if the pure, true prophecy pointed to the purely spiritual realm of justice; as if there could be a purely spiritual justice without application to things and times. If justice is really spirit it must prove itself as justice *in matter*; otherwise it is unreal justice and therefore not justice at all; it has become non-justice. The Spirit is then made ineffective, is made non-spirit.

In strong contrast to this empty concept, it was the conviction of the Jewish prophets that the Spirit shall be poured out over this earth; that sons and daughters of the earth shall speak and work in the Spirit; that all strata of earth's inhabitants, gripped by this Spirit, shall announce and live out the practical, active love, the justice that applies to all things. When all men on earth are a unity of brothers in this Spirit, the cultivation of field and garden, the fertility of the earth in undreamed-of wealth will open up a new civilization for the transformed city as well, a civilization that brings peace and life community to all men. This was the faith of the prophets for earth and its mankind.

The crucial element in this faith was the clear knowledge that this revolution of all things, this creative new ordering of all earthly conditions can come only from God. For only He is the power of creation and new creation. Each new era of plants, each new era of animals and the era of mankind that followed them on this planet earth broke forth through the power of the infinite, vast Prime Cause. So too, this new, creative action, breaking forth out of the same source of power, inaccessible to us and impenetrable to our searching, will bring on the kingdom of justice and peace. We cannot make any creation. We cannot create a new creation. The development of things and men, if it could be made independent, cannot bring about any new kingdom of peace and justice. For this a different power is needed, and that is the same one power that brings the fixed stars and planets into being out of the primeval vapor. It is the power that forms the earth's crust out of this planet's glowing body; that upon this crust divides the waters above from the waters of the depths; the same power that brings into being in this water, on this earth, the first, simplest living beings; the same power that calls animals and men into being.

This is the very same power that brings about the new time of justice and peace. We are not this power. We cannot make either conditions on earth or men new and good. The prophetic message of the God to come, of the coming intervention by His power, the proclamation of the peace that He will bring, of the justice that He gives, contains the demand that man shall become new, because it bears within it the faith in God as its sole and final faith.

God is the future of men, even as He is their origin. He approaches us with His demand and His promise: Break up your fallow ground! Break new ground! Away with the old, petrified heart. You must have a heart of flesh and blood, stirred and filled with life and feeling. The Spirit must come over you as the rain comes over the dried out, sun-baked desert, cracked and fissured in its hardness. The Spirit who is God himself must give life to the dead bones of a mankind that has basically and actually died. The Spirit must enter into them; otherwise they will remain dead.

Mankind must turn around. What good are all their religious exercises, what good are all their worship services, what meaning is there in all their devout songs, if God's will is not done, if their hands are full of blood! What does all their believing signify if injustice is done to the poor as easily as one drinks a glass of water? What is the sense of confessing to God if not even a little finger is lifted at the death of countless children and poor?

Change completely! Turn around! Become different; become men. Believe God. Give your life to God. This is the prophets' message. This call has its final and single purpose in the knowledge of God. He breaks into our world like lightning into the night. He changes the earth and transforms its mankind. God is the sole meaning of all repentance. His rulership over everything is the purpose of all inner change. All prophets have proclaimed Him alone.

In John, the last prophet to arise among the Jews, this message attained its simplest greatness. John was an ascetic. He rejected the clothing of civilized people. He left their dwellings and cities. He went into uncultivated nature. There was no need for him to seek people; people sought him. One, two, ten, twenty, a hundred — large numbers of them came out to him. Out there, where there were no temples and palaces, no houses, no fields, no woods, he told them the truth. It was the truth of all prophets. "Change radically! The turning of all things is near. The new order of creation is coming. That which now rules the world will be abolished. Something utterly different will guide this world. God is coming. God's rulership has come near." The head of this prophet fell because by his truth he tried to interfere in the family life of the most influential despot.

Jesus went with him. They were friends, John and Jesus, two hard fighters for the truth. First Jesus took up John's message as His own. He said the same that John had said: "Repent; the kingdom of God is at hand." But He was able to express more. "Believe in the message of joy!" John had pointed to Jesus, saying that He had the secret of the message. Now He is here, the one who counts. What Jesus brought was the message and its reality — who God is, what His future is like and what the way is like that is in keeping with God's future.

God was the message, God, the living, the

ultimate reality. Jesus did not believe in that god who brings unhappiness and baseness upon men, death and its demons and bacilli, crime and its injustice. On the contrary, He confesses the God who eliminates all these things. He knows that in this world a fearful might of evil prevails. But He knows more: that it will be overcome, that everything will be completely new and different. The victory over the evil, deadly power in this world — this is the task of His life. The purpose of Jesus' mission is that the spirit of this earth, who is the tyrant over this earth to the present day, be dispatched and thrown out; that this strong spirit be stripped of his entire power; that his land be occupied by God, his achievements and works be destroyed; that the satanic realm of the present state of affairs cannot prevail.

This fact means that a power shall come over the earth that is different from anything that has importance on the earth today. This message promises the most radical new order of all things, including things political and social, cultural and agricultural, ethnographical and geographical. The new, different order of all things is the substance of Jesus' words. His will is always this one thing: May thy rulership break in! May everything else on this earth perish, so that no one shall prevail on this earth but thou. May that which thou art, God, which the earth until now has only blasphemed, at last become that which alone is consecrated. May thy will be what happens on earth, as it happens in heaven! Jesus described this new order as something that comes from heaven. In the heavenly world it already rules now as the unity of the universe and as the circling course of the stars, as light and life, as the harmony and law-governed spirituality of matter, as justice and peace. All this shall rule on this earth as well! That heaven come onto earth, that the earth itself become the kingdom of heaven — that is the goal.

All the parables of the heavenly kingdom point to this one goal. Let us think just of the one picture of a ruler who leaves on a journey and hands his realm over to his co-workers, entrusting to each one of them a certain part of the whole for their management. Now it is their task to work with the property entrusted to them in a way that will meet the conditions for his return. When he comes he will call them all to account to find whether they have used the powers entrusted to them to do the work in accordance with his will. When he returns he will hold a festive communal table — as for a wedding, his symbol of creation, fellowship, and joy in life — uniting all those who were determined and able to administer the earth as he wanted it done and to permeate it with his spirit.

They shall possess the earth, the land. In the Sermon on the Mount, those concentrated words about the character of God's people of the future, Jesus disclosed most deeply this innermost meaning of His message. In it He calls all those happy who realize that they need to receive; He calls all those happy who want nothing but justice; who work peace and goodness; who are determined, undivided and pure. These people He sends out as salt that halts final decomposition and decay, as light that shines into the midst of the night of darkness.

Unless you become so totally different that you begin life all over again like newborn babes, you can never enter the new order that is coming. Here you will never again kill, never again serve killing. This not-killing not only means that you will not take anybody's life under any circumstances, including war or revolution. It also means that you will make no resistance, will not stand on your rights, especially when people harass you and try to rob you of your goods and your life. And it means the whole of your heart; that you despise no one and degrade no one; that you know no anger, revenge or ill will against anybody. The character of the people of the future is to make peace and to have fellowship in all things.

Purity of faithfulness in marriage is the physical reality that symbolizes this love and goodness. If the covetous will for property and influence is still craving in you; if the desirous will for sexual possession flares up in you, even if only as a thought, a look, a gesture, then it would be better to tear out the eye, to cut off the hand, so as to live free of these things, than to go to ruin with all one's limbs.

In all things you must be whole and genuine; you must be as God wants you. The people of the future are simple and faithful, open and trustworthy. They keep their word once given, in love as well as in all other dealings; this is what their character must be. Let your speech be reliable and simple: yes when it must be yes, without any fuss, and no when it must be no.

Let your manner be unaffected, your words concise. Be equally plain and fully dedicated, in deed as in word. Perhaps you have believed until now that one can defend oneself, that in self-defense one should strike back; that one can lay claim to one's full rights and sue legally for a rightful possession. But I tell you the new. If someone sues you to take away a coat, give him your jacket as well. Once you begin to put love into practice, you will soon have no more occasion to possess anything for yourself. Give to all who ask you for anything. Total and genuine love for people will make love for possession fall away from you because it has become impossible.

This love cannot stop anywhere; it cannot be limited to those who are close to you. This love shall also be love for the furthest away; it will become love to your enemies.

For it is a question of God. It is a question of becoming like your Father in heaven, of willing the will that God wills, of becoming as God is. God lets His sun shine on the bad and the good, on those who slander Him and those who love

Him. And just as God works in secret, so you too will live in your smallness, your simplicity and your love, unknown and in stillness. Whoever spreads his own good deeds abroad does not belong to the men of the future. Whoever displays his relationship with God to the many, whoever lets others see his privations and his meditations, has lost the best part of his life. And anyone who cannot even carry out the basic law of truthfulness toward God, that is, conciseness in words and objective clarity in saying only what needs to be said, will be counted among the hypocrites rather than among the people of the future.

The greatest simplicity in everything, abstention from excessive bodily pleasures, including those connected with the instincts of self-preservation and propagation, so as to be able to live whole and undivided in dedicated love for everyone and everything — this is the character of the future. Here there is no sourness of mien, no moping in sham holiness; here people proclaim with radiant, happy and lively eyes that the essence of love is joy.

Only wholeness of will can go such a way. Anyone who still hankers with half his heart for the illusion of wealth cannot enter this way. Nor can all those poor go this way who with half of their will, in worry and envy, yearn for possessions they do not have. No one can serve two masters. You cannot serve God and Mammon. You cannot serve God and at the same time struggle for livelihood and property. You cannot serve God and live in care. You can recognize and love God only when your whole longing, your innermost drive, your entire will and all the practical work you do is turned to the one single thing. This one thing is the coming Kingdom, the coming overturning of all things, the love of justice for all, God's lordship in the future, God and His will. Strive only for God's sovereignty over all things. Seek to live the life which alone counts as good under His rulership. Whatever you need to do, it will be given to you.

Anyone who is struck and gripped thus by God cannot possibly continue to assess other people's character or mode of life as worse than the things in himself that obstruct true life. Here there is no more judging. The gravity of one's own antagonism to God and the indissoluble link between one's personal guilt and the public collective guilt preclude untruthful, disrespectful condemning of others just as much as they preclude that other, related impudence: pious conduct and ostentatious talk. What is holy must be shielded from the shameless clutch of desecrating hands. The holy must not be profaned. Faith and love shall not become idle talk. The highest things are threatened with corruption from all sides.

You must tremble when you are told to knock at the door of truth and to live truth. You must go through a dangerously narrow door. You must walk on a perilous ridge. Leave everything outside and below. Thin, narrow, steep, stony and precipitous, the ascent leads past one abyss after another. At this seemingly unattainable distance, one basic demand for the daily practical life of our time can be seen by everyone: Whatever you would like to expect from others, give the same to them. The necessities of life that you work for and strive to get for yourselves, the necessary things you try to achieve for yourselves, whatever you feel you need to build up your own lives rightly—obtain these things for all men! Do for everyone what you want for yourselves.

The predacious nature, the killing nature,
appears in the desire for acquiring and clinging
to possessions. The men of the future are not
those who are able to say, "Lord, Lord," but
only those who act with all their will. Those
who work and produce — these are the ones
who have surrendered their daily actions to the
will of love. The main point is to do God's will,
to put His love into practice in work. Anyone
who has an active part in injustices, in social
wrong, whether in publicly responsible pro-
fessional work or in the smallest personal circle,
is rejected by Jesus as one with whom He has
never had anything to do.

Jesus therefore closes His prophetic account
of the people of God with a metaphor of decision. Either we erect the building of our life on
a slippery, sliding surface, such as elevating
feelings, pious rituals, clever theories or empty
words about politics or religion — the structure
of such a life must end in a frightful catastrophe
— or we build our life upon a foundation firmly
and deeply established, like a craggy fortress
that grows up out of rock. Then let come what
will. The storms of the times may pass over us;
everything that we perhaps consider a vital

necessity today may be taken away from us. Enmity and unjust judgment may come to us. It will be impossible to destroy the building of such a life. This building is nothing but the simple willing and doing of what God wants and what God is.

Only those who in trust do the will of the Father, who with all their will and action put their trust in God who comes from the heavens, will be able to find their way into God's new order.

This is the crucial secret of the Sermon on the Mount: that this life of trust is like the living growth of a tree, like the essence of salt, like the radiating warmth of the light sacrificing itself; that this gift is growth in the sense of being and becoming. Only the living tree bears fruit. Where the tree is, there is the fruit. Where the fruit is, there is the tree.

THE JESUS OF THE FOUR GOSPELS

IT HAS BECOME CLEAR to us that we as a church community, as a renewal of the original Christian church in Jerusalem, have to hold to Jesus. It is of utmost importance that we place the Jesus of the four Gospels, the Son of Mary, who was executed under Pontius Pilate, in the center of our faith and our life, and keep to Him. This Jesus has become completely unknown; His words have been distorted and disfigured; His work has been weakened. This is the Jesus who must be newly discovered, whom we must hold up before all the world.

We cannot live our common life in any other way than oriented by the life, the word and the work of Jesus. What is laid upon us is the love of Christ which is poured into our hearts by the Holy Spirit. This love does not contain the unclarity of human thoughts or feelings. In Jesus' life it has been made completely and unmistakenly clear. Through the Holy Spirit the power of this life of Jesus was poured out on the first church in Jerusalem. This life was sealed as the revelation of God's heart by His death and resurrection. And through the Holy Spirit this sealing of the life of Jesus was communicated to the church so that it might follow Him and carry His life anew into this world.

Of this Spirit Jesus foretold that He would remind the church of all the words Jesus had spoken during His life. Within the church the Spirit would show this same life of Jesus in the clearest light and through it reveal the whole future of God's kingdom. Further, in the mission of the church, the Spirit would convict and convince the world in regard to sin, righteousness, and judgment.

Jesus also said that these things, sin, righteousness, and judgment, would become visible in Him, in Jesus. Sin is to be shown by the Holy Spirit as the absence of belief in Jesus. Righteousness is to be shown by the Holy Spirit in the fact that Jesus has occupied the throne of God and that now from the ruling throne of God's kingdom He will bring the rule of righteousness on earth. Judgment is to be revealed through the Holy Spirit when the prince of this world, the spirit of the age that rules everywhere over all peoples, the god of this world, the spirit that is active in all unbelieving men, is judged by Jesus; judged, not through a powerful action of legions of angel princes over this violent Satan, but by the perfect love of Jesus Christ, revealed on the cross. Through this love He won the victory over Satan, not because He was more powerful and violent, but because He was better and more loving.

Jesus was shown to be the best and most loving one who could ever be known. In His living and in His dying, the goodness and love of God's heart was revealed in such a way as it never could have been in any other place or at any other moment. This means that from now on whoever takes Jesus' side and is gripped by His perfect love will be free from the judgment on the spirit of the earth, the spirit of the age, that rules this world as its god and its authority. But he who wants to follow the prince of this world and the prevailing spirit of this age that governs man, will be subject to the judgment together with the prince of the abyss, the earth spirit. For he follows the injustice of Mammon, the falseness and deceit and unfaithfulness of the evil spirit; he follows the murderous spirit of the abyss, and therefore he stands under judgment, just as the prince of this world is himself judged.

He who follows Jesus and believes in Him, however, has left the destructive fury of the devil's works. He who follows Jesus and believes in Him will not be judged, for he is already judged. A judgment by the spirit of the church has taken place and constantly takes place in his heart and his life and on the old Adam in him. It is judgment in the new sense of grace: that into the midst of this healing judgment true renewal and bestowal are given by the Spirit of Jesus Christ. Wherever there is the real church of Jesus Christ, through the outpouring of the Holy Spirit, this Holy Spirit rules. And where He rules, He reigns as the revelation of Jesus Christ, disclosing the victorious all-encompassing future of Jesus, and bringing it directly to the gathered believers.

All this is made known through the outpouring of the Holy Spirit in the church, just as it was made known by Jesus' actual life.

The outpouring of the Holy Spirit can bring with it no other content than the very content of Jesus' life. For Jesus is and remains the same, yesterday, when He was the Son of Mary; today, while He is being manifested to His church by the Holy Spirit; and tomorrow, when He will enter upon and prevail in His rule as King of God's kingdom.

The life of Jesus in all His actions and all His words has disclosed the ultimate mystery of God as perfect love. First of all we have to recognize that the Son of Mary is himself perfect love. We have to recognize that His love is perfect love for God. Love can only come from where its source is. God himself is the source of all love. It is not we who loved Him first; He loved us first by giving His Son for all of us.

The life and actions of Jesus and His completed work bring this love of God directly to us. His life, being God's love, shows itself as love for God. God's love is the love that proceeds from God; and it is the love of the believer for God himself. Out of this love was born everything that Jesus said and did. That He accepted the baptism of John and in this baptism con-

secrated himself to death already shows clearly
that He wanted to carry out God's whole
righteousness out of love for God, even to His
sacrifice on the cross. And when He went out
among men He proclaimed that which alone
moved and determined His heart: *The kingdom
of God is at hand.* What is important is God.
God must come to the fore. He alone must rule.
He shall conquer all. Everything shall come into
His realm and under His sway. The kingdom of
God is near!

Before Jesus went out to make this call to the
world, He had to fight the prince of this world.
His love to God proved victorious in the threefold temptation of Satan. The spirit of the
earth, being the prince of this world, offered
Him the conquest of all the world's thrones, of
all the great states, if only He would unite with
Satan, with the spirit of Mammon, of lying and
impurity and mass murder. Then He would not
need to go such a long way through cross and
resurrection, through outpouring of the Spirit
and founding of the church, and the last judgment. Then the whole world could be taken over
immediately by Jesus ruling in conjunction with
the prince of this world.

The tempter went further and demanded that Jesus proclaim His own greatness, that He show how great He was as the Son of man, that He manifest himself in a powerful supremacy over the laws of nature. Satan wanted Jesus to triumph over the laws of nature in front of all the people as the greatest man of all. He wanted Him to use the weapon of demagoguery to win the people by impressing them with His power and might. This power of suggestion over the people was to be exploited further by giving them plenty of bread, in a place where there was no bread at all. All this He was to do through an inner union with the spirit that worked against God in this world, both before and after the coming of Jesus.

But Jesus loved His Father above all else. He was not concerned with the rulership of any kingdom; He was not concerned with having the whole earth at His command. He was not concerned with winning a huge following among the masses. His concern was not to win men for himself. His sole concern was love to God. So He put Satan to flight. Away with thee, Satan! I will serve none but God alone. Man lives not only by bread and food for the body; he lives much more by every fiery word born of God's breath, which has its life from God's loving heart.

It was to bring this word of God's heart in among men that Jesus came. To represent and spread the worship and honor of this heart of God among men — this is why He wanted God's kingdom. This story of the temptation shows most clearly what fearful dangers prowl around each human heart, and in particular every human heart that has been met by a higher call. Before Jesus proclaimed, "The kingdom of God is at hand," men had to be called to repent, to change their whole way of thinking, to overthrow completely their entire previous lives. Change your lives radically in every way, prepare for the coming Kingdom, by turning upside down everything you have hitherto felt, thought and done.

The supreme event is imminent, compared to which all other events in the history of mankind mean nothing. Now God comes to men. Now history among men really starts. True, there has been preparatory history. But only now does the real history begin, the history that brings decision and changes all things. For the kingdom of God is coming. For this you must prepare yourselves. Therefore the one decisive call to you is: Love God! Change so much that you will be able to love with your whole hearts. Change your lives so that everything you do will be nothing but love to Him. Change in such a way that this love to God will not only be a personal matter of your hearts, but so that this love will mean for you the revolution of all things, the removal of all injustice and the conquest of all countries and all peoples for His reign.

You are constantly under the powerful influence of the beast of prey that prowls around you pretending to be an angel of light, claiming that on its way everything will become gradually better. Therefore you must change your thinking, change it completely, so that you cannot succumb to this seductive influence. You must be able to believe only in one sole message of joy and utterly reject every other. You shall believe only in this one joyful news: God is near! His rule breaks in! You cannot expect any good of anything else. This is your new thinking, this is the change in the whole direction of your lives. Believe in this message, this news, this gospel!

Jesus not only proclaimed the gospel in these brief words of the call to repentance. Nor did He only bring it home to people by a wealth of parables. Nor did He only present in symbolic deeds and miracles its actual presence among men. He also represented the substance of this message in clear, unequivocal language. We are to know with certainty that the Spirit of God is coming, that His rule is approaching.

In the talk with Nicodemus at the beginning of the Gospel of John, Jesus says that to recognize, to behold this Kingdom, to become incorporated into it, is possible only through a complete new beginning of human life. When a child is born, something completely new comes into our midst. This child was not there. We know nothing about this child yet except that it is here now and beginning its life. This is exactly how the new beginning should be which is necessary in order to behold and enter the kingdom of God. The individual must be so renewed that he begins his life right from the start, like a newborn child. He must be born quite new.

This new birth takes on a definite meaning. Just as a child is born into a family, and here into a church community, like the little baby born today, so the new birth of the spirit, the rebirth of man, means that man is born into the kingdom of God. The surroundings into which he is born, that which he sees from the hour of his new birth, is God's kingdom and nothing but God's kingdom. Do not be surprised that you have to be born again; for without this new birth you cannot see the kingdom of God. Without this new birth you cannot enter the kingdom of God. What is at stake in this new birth is the kingdom of God. That which is most subjective is here the most objective.

In the Gospel of Matthew the mystery of this new birth, the vision of this new world into which the child is born, is most clearly described. At the beginning of this Gospel comes the Sermon on the Mount, which shows us the nature and character of this new life of rebirth for the kingdom of God. It shows what one actually sees and beholds when one gains the new life; it shows what kind of world one is born into if one is truly reborn. The new life brings a justice that cannot be compared with any human morality, any human social order or human theology. The new life of rebirth brings a justice that is nothing but the goodness of God, nothing but the good heart of God. This justice is therefore better than anything ever thought, felt, willed, or said by men; for this new justice is God's own doing.

The new righteousness is the outpouring of God's Spirit. The new righteousness is the essence of His innermost life. It is the blazing up of His coming light. The new righteousness is the saltiness of salt. It is God's nature, His essence and substance, His basic working; and so it is the most vital life, the freest mobility and activity. For this new righteousness is life born out of God and therefore utterly opposed to every kind of self-righteousness, every kind of human righteousness. Self-righteousness and human righteousness begin with self-confidence, with making claims and demands for human justice. But divine justice — the new righteousness — begins by becoming a beggar, becoming poor and being judged; it begins by extinguishing all claims to possessions, all rights and privileges.

Further, the new justice begins by taking on the load of all the need and suffering of the whole world. It is the beginning of the new

justice when suffering lies, with all the heaviness
of the world, on the human heart, on the believing heart. True, human justice also knows
something of compassion with the world, but
this justice immediately turns into hatred,
bloodthirsty hatred against those who have
caused that suffering. Thus it becomes injustice,
because among the guilty — and in fact all men
are guilty — it seeks out a group of particularly
guilty people to fight against them with fierce
hatred.

The justice of the new kingdom of Jesus
Christ desires God's universal peace in the
midst of lovelessness and unpeace. It desires
the goodness and the love which has a heart
for all men, including the guiltiest. It feels mercy
for all men, even for those who have sinned most
severely against peace and justice. For this new
righteousness, this righteousness of God, reveals
itself as the heart of God which is ready for
sacrifice, ready for death. It is the will that does
not want to kill the guilty but rather to be killed
for the guilty, so that they may become innocent
by grasping the deepest meaning and value of
this sacrifice of love; by recognizing and ex-
periencing God and His heart in this readiness

for sacrifice till the last drop of blood. God can be found only if one is prepared to suffer death for His righteousness and His kingdom. Our physical life, the last thing we men have and try to cling to, even this last right and privilege must be ready for sacrifice. Only then are we truly reborn for the kingdom of God.

At the beginning of the Sermon on the Mount, Jesus opened the way to the understanding of the kingdom of God. The rest then follows as it must follow out of this root which is the innermost nature of God: Now, enemies are loved. For love's sake one surrenders the last possessions, one gives the last coat, the last cloak, the last shirt. Now one does not pay back force with force. One does not resist evil by responding with evil. Here is faithfulness, and in faithfulness purity, including human physical and emotional relationships. Here is the only good, the truly better righteousness; it is the revelation of perfect love, of eternal loyalty in love, and therefore also in the inviolable marriage between two people. You shall in your way be as perfect as the Father himself is perfect. In your words too you shall be perfect, in that you say nothing superfluous, but speak the truth

simply, clearly, and to the point. There is no
other truthfulness than that of love; there is no
other perfection than that of love.

In Jesus' next words it becomes clear what is
the nature of the things that thwart and destroy
love. It is Mammon. You cannot serve God and
Mammon at the same time. You cannot serve
ownership and love at the same time. Nor can
you serve material worries and at the same time
serve trusting love. Whoever heaps up property
or holds on to even the smallest private property
for his own interest, while his brothers and
fellow men are hungry and cold and can't keep
a roof over their heads, has no love. Therefore
Jesus says, do not gather property, have nothing
at all belonging to yourselves, have no hidden
treasures or reserves anywhere.

But do not worry about your livelihood,
either. This fear about being provided for, seeks
just as anxiously to preserve the material basis
for life as the man who wants to hold on to his
bank account or his real estate. All this belongs
to Mammon just as much as the retaining of
property. Grey, foggy worry is born of the
spirit of Mammon just as much as golden,
glittering money. Therefore do not worry. Learn

from nature, which you should love because it is God's creation. Look at the birds and flowers. Believe in the loving Father, who sets their table for them and gives them their feathers and colorful raiment.

The righteousness of the kingdom of God, the renewal of the reborn heart, means singleness of heart, an eye concentrated on God alone. The heart of man can be compared to an inner eye which is focused and concentrated on one single object, an eye of concentric vision. The focus of this inner eye is God alone.

If your inner eye is really concentrated on God alone, you cannot have any fortune, nor can you have any worries either. Instead you will grasp that to call upon God is to trust in His love; to call on God is to implore His rulership. It is the doing of His will, the hallowing of His name. It is the gift of daily bread, spiritual as well as temporal. With this single eye, you will have new loving hearts, free from evil and the rule of violence, free from the temptation that will shake even the last hour of this world. In *this* way call upon God.

This love to God means love to all men; for God loves all men and His heart is directed

toward all men. He is merciful to all and lets
His sun shine on all and gives His rain to all.
Therefore a man who through the love of God
has experienced new birth cannot judge any
other man; rather he must have faith for all
men. Jesus says, do not judge men; love them.
Judgment means passing a final, conclusive
verdict. This you must never do. Love's hope
and faith's trust must always leave open the
way to return home, to be saved for God's
kingdom.

For the sake of the love you have for God,
however, beware of surrendering the holiest
thing that lives in your hearts to men who are
not ready for it. For then you would be aban-
doning true love to God in favor of a sham love.
Speak to men as befits their inner receptiveness,
in a way they can grasp; but do so without
denying the least grain of the truth. Either of
these would be a sin against love for God — to
judge men, or to share indiscriminately what is
holy with people who are unawakened. Either
would be a sin against love, love to God and to
men.

Know that God's love is always greater than
your judgment and your opinion. God's love is

always purer and more inviolable than that which you call love.

God alone knows the hearts of men; He knows the hearts of the guilty and the innocent in their depths. Therefore pray for the Spirit that comes from God's heart, so that in your dealings with men you may have that wisdom which you can never receive from yourselves.

One piece of advice I must give you. Deal with all men as you wish them to treat you. You wish for yourselves that God may care for you in body, soul, and spirit. And what you expect for yourselves you should make possible for all men. And this should be done without exceptions. This is the new righteousness. You must not limit the good works of your love to people congenial to you; for God loves all men, no matter what they are like. Therefore you too, love all men with the love that is of God, and do to them everything that you wish done to you and yours.

The genuine love, the new justice that is for *all* — this is the truth of God's kingdom. The Biblical advice to treat all men as you would like them to treat you and your family — this is the narrow gate through which you must enter.

This new justice is better than that of all the moralists and theologians. It is the narrow mountain path, the entry into the kingdom of God, the ascent to the city on the hill. Love men as you love yourselves; love them because you love God and because you have experienced that God loves all men. You accept that you are cared for in body and soul and spirit; therefore you must make the same possible for all men. Only then will you know the door to the kingdom of God; only then will you know the narrow path along the abyss, that leads up to the city of God.

There will be very few of you beginning *now* to go this way. Troublesome spirits and violent hostile powers will oppose you. Their outward violence will be able to do little harm to you, for it cannot kill your conscience or change your will. More dangerous is false prophecy that joins forces with this violence and tries to confuse the single eye. Therefore it is necessary for you to recognize false prophecy. You will know it by its deeds, above all by this one sign of its nature, whether it takes sides with the beast of prey or not. Everything that is connected with the savage nature of Mammon, with unfaithful physical passion, with the shedding of blood, with lying business methods, is false prophecy. Everything that falls in with the rapacious nature of collective egotism is false prophecy. Beware of the veiled nature of the wild beast.

Love the true prophet. You will know him by what his love is. This love can ultimately be recognized in that the true prophet gives his life for his beloved brothers. The readiness to sacrifice one's own physical life, without injuring any other life — this is the mark of true prophecy.

We have seen how Jesus disclosed in the Sermon on the Mount the character of the new way of life and the new kingdom; how He showed the nature of the new building of life that cannot collapse, that cannot be corrupted by any worldly power, how by the content of this Sermon He proclaimed the truth everywhere and ever again.

Very soon a powerful enmity to Jesus arose. His opponents beset Him with cunning cleverness and sought to trip Him in intellectual discussions. They tried to bring Him to the point where they would have grounds for killing

Him, grounds that would be valid in the eyes of the people and the government. For even the beast of prey has to be clever. Even the false prophets have to be clever. They must not allow evil directly to appear evil; they have to cloak it with goodness. Therefore they sought a cause which would be sufficient for the whole people and the conscience of the government to recognize Jesus as guilty and condemn Him to death.

The leading classes of the people, and an increasingly large part of the common people too, rejected Jesus more and more the longer He worked, especially after He had sent out His twelve, two by two, and His seventy, two by two, giving them mighty authority. After they had come back without having won the people of Israel for the kingdom of God, Jesus made a tremendous decision. He withdrew to His parables. These parables were meant to veil the truth to the obtrusive, in order not to deliver what was holy to the beasts of prey. At the same time the parables were to show the truth all the more deeply to those who really wanted to hear. Those who wanted to hear something with false hearts only to be able to contradict it afterwards were to run up against an impenetrable wall in these parables. In fact, up to the present day no human theology, no false prophecy has ever been able to understand these parables.

To open hearts, however, the church was to be opened up. Here the ultimate meaning of the message of God's kingdom was shown. In the first place it was revealed in the parable of unity, that of the wedding and the supper — the deepest unity possible among men and the most inclusive and yet most intimate fellowship of the table possible among men. Complete uniting and the fellowship of many at one table — this is the mystery of the kingdom of God. But this wedding feast, this supper is seen in connection with the King and the King's Son, so that it may be recognized that this fellowship of God's kingdom among men is not a value in itself; it receives its value only because it is the King who holds this wedding and who invites people to this supper.

The kingdom of God is compared with the royal wedding and with the royal supper. Later parables show us that this unity consists not only in the joy of uniting, but also in the creative activity of this uniting. Therefore Jesus likens

the kingdom of God to the work in the vineyard,
and in another place to the worker who does
yes while saying no. Real unity and community
are present only where there is common work,
for love is deed. And if we ask what this deed is,
then the parables of Jesus show us that this
deed is utmost surrender; it is work directed
toward the future, work entirely dependent on
the blessing of heaven. The sower is likened to
the kingdom of God, and so is the farmer who
waits for the right weather, and so is the field
in which the crop is intermingled with weeds
deceptively similar to it.

Total readiness for God's kingdom means
work in united love and at the same time a
believing and loving expectation of God, that
He will bring all things to their completion.
The new cannot be patched on to the old
garment of old religious and social strivings. On
the contrary, everything one had before must
be given away for the one jewel — the kingdom
of God. All earthly possessions must be sold
and left behind. This is the only way to the
kingdom of God. Even all old ideals must be
left behind if we are to walk on the only road to
the kingdom of God.

This is a decision that is very hard for people to make. For at first the kingdom of God works only like a leaven. The bread is the whole world of all peoples and all men, and the leaven of truth is worked into the midst of these peoples of all mankind. The kingdom of God is like a small grain of seed which is one day to become a big bush but at present is still in process of growing, still insignificant. One day there shall be a great world tree under which all will find their shelter and dwelling. But now it is only a small, insignificant seed. The significance of this seed is that it is really alive; it has the aliveness of the tree of God, that mighty living tree under whose branches everything shall be united and all may live and dwell.

But opposing this growth there is a terrible enemy power which imitates everything that God allows to grow, sowing weeds among the pure seed. The true readiness of faith does not allow itself to be disquieted by this. It does not uproot the weeds; it does not allow itself to be rushed into any violent action. It lets both grow till the time of harvest, the hour when God himself will intervene. The faith of readiness never allows itself to be betrayed into an unbelieving zeal for violence. The kingdom of Christ never uses the means of the kingdom of Satan; it knows that it has to disarm Satan in his innermost chamber, where he develops his most secret power. This is the place of death and the place of sin, which is the weapon of death. The kingdom of Christ can never take into its own hands this weapon struck out of Satan's hands. It is free of all means involving violence and deceit. It is a kingdom of pure love and thereby a kingdom of complete victory.

These parables show clearly something that was already evident in the Sermon on the Mount: the character which the comrades of God's kingdom, the citizens of the city of God, must have. The nature of their strength is their fundamental character. Like rocks and trees they are unshakable in all storms and all floods, and like fertile trees they bear abundant fruit. This fruit is ever the same — love and joy, unity and surrender in unity, innermost readiness and gathering for God's kingdom.

It is made clear that the tree must not be unfruitful, otherwise it will be felled. The servant must not be merciless, otherwise he will be excluded from the household. Whoever in a loveless way tries to take the first place at the meal of unity, the fellowship of the table, must be sent out. Whoever does not want to wear a festive garment has to leave the dining room. Whoever is loveless to his fellow servants has to be put outside.

What is decisive then, in the parables as well, is love to men and readiness for the coming of God. This we see in the parable of the ten virgins — the five who were completely ready, through the Spirit, and the other five who were only half ready, without the Spirit. We see it also in the persevering calling and pleading of the friend at the window, in the child who pleads with his father. Readiness means a persevering faithfulness, a watchful, steady call; this we see also in the faithful steward and the loyal servant, in the administrators, who must be persevering and alert in keeping faithfully the things entrusted to them. We see it also in the parable of the talents, the entrusted goods. These have to be held and utilized fully and faithfully. Everyone who is not faithful and firm until the end will some day find a locked door. Everybody should know beforehand that such a structure, such a campaign, can only be carried through when one stakes everything for it, when all powers are used to finish the building and to see the fight through to the end.

The nature of the citizens of the city of God is that of active, persevering love. Here no one favors his own well-being. The parable of poor Lazarus shows us clearly, not that the rich man was an exceptional usurer; his only object was to enjoy his riches. Out of his abundance he gave plenty of alms to the poor, unhappy beggar lying on his door step. And yet he had nothing to do with the kingdom of God, because he enjoyed the greatest part of his riches for himself and gave away only a little of his surplus. That is impossible in the kingdom of God. Here is only the humble heart that surrenders everything it has and is; that lets itself be redeemed from its own conceit, from all that is self, as shown in the parable of the Pharisee and the publican. Only the one who can say, "O God, have mercy on me, a poor sinner," belongs to God's kingdom. But if he is still able to say, "How happy I am that I am not like that man," he does not belong to God's kingdom any more than that foolish rich man who when he had filled up all his barns thought, "I had better build another barn," and in the same night he was dead.

Wealth, both in material goods and in one's own morality, closes the door to God's kingdom. This is shown by the parables of the lost sheep, of the prodigal son, and of the coin sought so long in vain. The son who had gone astray and become quite poor was the very one who received the greater love when he returned, willing to surrender himself completely to the household, even in the lowest place. The lost sheep, dirtier and weaker than the others, was sought with special love and reincorporated into the community of the flock. The lost coin was sought for a longer time and was the cause of more concern than the others that had remained in the cash box.

All this is said, not to raise the value of the individual, but rather to recognize that even the most lost, the dirtiest, the loneliest, most isolated and furthest away — all these shall be brought into the fellowship, into the kingdom of God, into uniting, into usefulness for the whole, for all, before the door of the father's house, the sheep pen or the drawer is closed. Ultimately it is not a question of the one sheep, the one lost son, the one coin. What matters is the return to

the true flock, the uniting of the flock with the
true Shepherd, unity in the true pasture. Then
real fellowship will arise, and love for the
individual and for the whole will be revealed as
love for God.

The whole mystery of God's kingdom is like
a landscape or a big plantation where everything belongs together. It is organic unity and
concord and community. This organic unity is
like a vine, a plant, in which Christ himself and
His Holy Spirit is the love, the power and the
binding force of life.

If we grasp the parables in this way, we will
understand why Jesus also said those words
about the splinter and the beam. People are
always glad to tell someone else what he has
done wrong; and we ought to help one another.
But this is possible only if the big piece of wood
is first removed from our own eye, so that the
smaller piece of wood may also be removed. It
is we ourselves who must be purified for the
innermost character of God's kingdom.

After these parables Jesus went to the attack
once more.

The love of Jesus is complete love; just
because of this it is not a soft love. It rejects

evil and fights it to the last, whether it be a
beam or a splinter in the eye. Therefore Jesus
calls out His sevenfold "Woe!" over the false
prophets. For the same reason, in announcing
the terrible judgment He proclaims the catastrophe of the last days of this world. His last
speeches glow with the certainty that a fearful
judgment of fire must come over this earth and
mankind because they do not allow themselves
to be won by His love, but persist in their
heartlessness and enmity to God. It became
evident through Jesus' life that this was men's
attitude. He was executed as an enemy of men,
an enemy of the best state and the best church.

Everything that Jesus said, He did as well.
The life of Jesus is the doing of His love and
the living out of His entire proclamation. Everything He had proclaimed in the Sermon on the
Mount and in His parables He put into practice
in gathering His twelve disciples into a community of goods and a fellowship of wandering,
in the homelessness and loving surrender of this
common life. And He further put it into practice
in sending out these disciples of His who, as
God's true ambassadors of the coming kingdom,
were to represent the full authority and the

complete love of the kingdom of God in their mission.

Jesus proved His sustaining power and the wonder of His strength for community in the way He endured in community with His disciples, who were often so foolish, right to the end — until *they* fled while He was crucified. He proved it in the way He carried out this common life in faithful instruction and teaching of His disciples, passing on His truth to them until the end.

The four Gospels, from which we have this understanding of Jesus' life, were written a long time after Jesus' death. But they were written as the outcome of the daily teaching of Jesus and of the continuation of these teachings in the church of Jesus. These stories of Jesus Christ were told and retold whenever the church of Jesus gathered among the early Christians, later among the Waldensians, among our [Anabaptist] Brothers, and many others. Man needs reminders; his memory needs refreshing. Through this oral transmission of the stories of Jesus, through the joy of telling over and over again who Jesus was, what He did and said, the truth was carried from heart to heart, from one life into another.

At the end of the Gospel of John, he says that Jesus did many other things, but that if they were all to be written down, the world could not hold the books that would have to be written. But those deeds which were recorded show us very clearly the inmost content of His life and all His authority. What He did within His own circle was nothing else than what He spoke and proclaimed. It was an expression of the love to which body, soul, and spirit alike give themselves. His deeds proved what that was to be which He proclaimed.

In the driving out of demons and diabolic powers it is shown most powerfully that the rule of God's kingdom is present when devils are driven out of human bodies by the finger of the Holy Spirit. So too, the healings of the sick show that death and its root in sin were eliminated by the coming of Jesus and the approach of God's kingdom. For the spirit of death is the ultimate enemy of the spirit of life. Death is the last enemy of God.

Therefore Jesus heals the sick. He heals those who suffer from dangerous skin diseases, from leprosy, those who have lost one of their faculties, such as the blind and the deaf. He heals those who have lost their life strength because of internal disease. He heals paralytics who as a consequence of licentious living have lost the strength of their bones. He heals persons with a withered arm or with fever. He makes the deaf hear again and the dumb speak again. He lifts up stunted bodies and heals sick people who have been waiting in vain for years for a miraculous healing. Once He healed someone whose physical health had been impaired by one of His own disciples. He also healed a relative of His disciple Peter, his mother-in-law, who was suffering from a fever. He heals people with dropsy, people who are dying.

By all this He proves that the power of the devil is not a purely emotional matter. By these healings of the sick Jesus wants to show that the devil is a power that infects and destroys — and this includes the body. Wherever Jesus intervenes, this destructive power is beaten back and bodies are regained for the honor of God and the holiness of His name.

Therefore Jesus cannot stop even before death; for death is the most severe sickness, and all other sicknesses are nothing but the pains that precede death. Death is the last weapon of the satanic power. Therefore Jesus turns to people who have died. He even raises back to life persons whose bodies were already in a state of decay. He touches corpses. The dead are awakened through the intervention of Jesus Christ. He had to prove the power of life against death itself. Without resurrection, without the raising of the dead, the news of God and His life would be null and void. Therefore the fact of Jesus' power to awaken is a central reality of His life and His gospel.

But Jesus does not stop with the things that concern human bodies. His deeds go further. When He fed the four thousand and the five thousand, and when He created wine at the wedding of Cana, these were still ways of helping men's bodies. So was the miraculous fishing in the Lake of Gennesaret. But when Jesus stilled the storm that raged over this same lake, when He made the fig tree wither, He showed that all the other elements of creation, too, must be touched by His breath and the approach of His kingdom. He showed that He rules all the elements of creation; that everything must be transformed into that completely new thing which is coming.

Everything Jesus did in His full authority points toward the end of days and to the beginning of God's kingdom. His deeds show that when God and His rule approach, a final miracle is to happen to the nature of the first creation too, to the bodies of men created and born. They show that God's love turns not only toward the inner man's soul, but just as much to his outer being, to the structure of nature as a whole.

Certainly it is decisive what happens in an inner way to the individual; for otherwise the individual has no part in the renewal of all things. But God's great interest is directed toward all creation, the entire nature of all worlds, so that they may all be included in this new creation which is the kingdom of God. Certainly the individual shall and must stop doing evil when his body is healed. Certainly the authority to forgive sins will become visible; the removal of evil in each individual will come into force, if the healing of the body and the proclamation of God's kingdom are to be his. The power of evil must be cleared out of the human heart. But this shall not happen so that the individual can be saved, but so that he can become free from himself for the mighty work which comes to this earth and takes hold of all in the approach of God's kingdom.

The works of the devil shall be destroyed. The creation, which through the evil influence of Satan was spoiled, shall be restored to the full aliveness God intended from the very beginning. Everything that happens is a sign and a symbol of the greatness that is to come when the invincible life of the second creation shall be manifest; when even death, the last enemy, shall be vanquished; when God shall rule as the creative Spirit of the new nature.

This mystery had to be revealed in Jesus himself. For this He truly rose and was revealed as the living one. He, the Risen One, is present in the church through the pouring out of the Holy Spirit. The experience of this pouring out of the Spirit in the church is the fulfilment of the words: I am with you always, till the end of the world. All authority in heaven and on earth has been given to me. Here, in the Holy Spirit, the King of the coming kingdom is present. The Spirit of the church is the presence of the King who conquers all worlds for God. The Holy Spirit, being the substance of life in the church, is the certainty of the joyful gospel that Jesus shall come as the King of the final kingdom.

And so we close with this last vision of the church in the Revelation of John, in which the voice from heaven reveals the end: Blessed and holy is he who partakes of the first resurrection; over him the second death has no power.

APPENDIX

Not a New Law was a talk during a meeting on October 27, 1935 at the Rhön Bruderhof. Several other chapters in this book, *To Become True Men, The Spirit of Life Overcomes, Joyful News of the Kingdom,* and *The Jesus of the Four Gospels* are, like this one, taken from stenographic notes of meetings in the Bruderhof community and translated for the present volume.

Leo Tolstoy, in his book *My Religion,* listed these five "new laws" of Jesus from the Sermon on the Mount in the fifth chapter of Matthew: to be at peace with everyone (verses 21-26); absolute sexual purity, faithfulness in marriage (verses 27-32); non-swearing of oaths (verses 33-37); non-resistance to evil (verses 38-42); love for one's enemies (verses 43-48).

To Become True Men was spoken during a meeting with guests at the Rhön Bruderhof on

Sunday, September 22, 1935. Some of the guests spoke and Eberhard Arnold then responded.

Salt and Light was first printed in the periodical *Das Neue Werk*, 1920, as *Licht und Salz,* and later reprinted in *Der Pflug* and *The Plough*, Vol. III, No. 4, 1955, in German and English respectively, as the third article in the series, "Studies in the Sermon on the Mount." All three of these articles appear in a new translation for this volume.

Happiness has previously been printed in German only, as an article, *Das Glück*, in *Das Neue Werk*, 1920/21.

For Bible reference see: Romans 8.2; 8.35.

The Nature of the New Justice was printed in 1922 in *Das Neue Werk* under the title, *Die Bergrede, ein Zeugnis vom Osterkursus in Sannerz, 1922*. It was first given as a talk for perhaps twenty to thirty friends who met in the Easter days at the Sannerz community, as a study group, taking the Sermon on the Mount as their theme that year.

For Bible reference see: Luke 6.20 ff.;

Matthew 5.13-14; Luke 14.34-35; Romans 8.2; Matthew 3.2; Luke 11.13.

"But I Say to You..." was first printed as *Die bessere Gerechtigkeit* in *Das Neue Werk,* 1920, pages 409 ff., and later reprinted in *Der Pflug* and *The Plough*, Vol. III, No. 3, 1955, in German and English respectively, as the second article in the series, "Studies in the Sermon on the Mount."

Away from Compromise and Shadow was published in the periodical, *Wegwarte*, 1925, No. 10/11, as *Fort von Kompromis und Schatten.* This article closed a controversy in print which ran for several numbers in the same magazine. The stand of the little community at Sannerz for a life of love and peace and non-violence, making no compromise with evil, was attacked as impossibility and madness by the Protestant direction of the German Youth Movement. Heinrich Euler, of the Youth Movement in Baptist circles, and others representing this point of view, made such statements in previous articles in the *Wegwarte* as the following:

"Body and spirit are in opposition and can never be brought into harmony." "It is humbug and vapor to speak of a life of nonviolence in this age." "Guilt is the shadow of our conscience which comes from the light," and "Never yet has any man leaped over his own shadow."

The opponents of Sannerz spoke of non-compromise as "self-delusion, foolishness and madness," citing as examples that while it may be possible to avoid holding public office or resorting to law, everyone must pay taxes, or work for an employer who pays taxes, eat food on whose ingredients duties and taxes are levied by the state, and use money minted by the government. It is only a matter of *more*, or *less* compromise. The taking of life is justified "to save perhaps thousands of fellowmen"; such action is called "responsible sinning."

A certain Max Dressler, who had taken part in discussions at Sannerz and had also written in *Wegwarte*, while stressing forgiveness as the help needed to renew life in God, had stated that "the demands of Jesus are not really demands in the actual sense of the word," and that "one cannot speak of discipleship without compromise."

Eberhard Arnold bases his answer to these claims on the Sermon on the Mount and the First Letter of John. The movement referred to is the Christian Youth Movement.

For Bible reference see: Luke 7.47; 1 John 4.20; 1.10; 2.1-2; 3.6; 5.19; 1.5; Hebrews 12.4.

Against Bloodshed and Violence is a shortened translation of the article *Gegen Blut und Gewalt* published in *Das Neue Werk* on April 15, 1921, as a protest against the widespread rioting which took place in German cities at the time in connection with general elections. Radical working class groups clashed with extreme rightists, and government forces intervened. Those taking a stand for peace and non-violence were publicly attacked as "seducers" and "prophets of lying" even by so-called "Christian" publicists, while Communist and Nationalist papers were instigating murder and more violence.

Hermann Hesse, quoted at the end of the chapter, was a German writer and poet.

The Better Righteousness was printed in both German and English in *Der Pflug* and *The*

Plough, Vol. III, No. 2, 1955, as the first of a series of three articles on the Sermon on the Mount, the other two being *"But I Say to You..."* and *Salt and Light*. Like the other two articles, it had also appeared earlier in German. This one appeared in *Mitteilungen zur Förderung einer deutschen christlichen Studentenbewegung* (News to Promote a Christian Student Movement in Germany), April 1919, with the title *Die bessere Gerechtigkeit*.

For Bible reference see: Matthew 5.20; 5.48.

God or Mammon, printed in *Der Wahrheitszeuge* (The Witness to Truth), a German Baptist periodical, Cassel, July 1915, with the title, *Gott oder Mammon*, bears the earliest date of the chapters in this book. There is a wide span of years between this 1915 article by Eberhard Arnold and *Not a New Law*, some words he spoke in a meeting less than a month before his untimely death on November 22, 1935. His occupation with the Sermon on the Mount was as lifelong as it was profound and, above all, practical.

Werner Sombart, 1863-1941, was a German political economist and advocate of liberal social reforms favoring the working classes.

For Bible reference see: Matthew 4.9; 12.29; Luke 11.21-22; Colossians 2.13-15; 2 Corinthians 5.15; Romans 6.8; Colossians 3.2-3.

The next three chapters, *How Can Men Fight Mammon?*, *God Mammon and the Living God*, and *The Decision*, were all given at different times as lectures, all bearing originally the same title, *Der Gott Mammon*.

How Can Men Fight Mammon? and *The Decision* were both part of a series of four lectures under the general heading, *Der Weg zum wahren Menschentum* (The Way to True Humanity). Neither has been published or translated previously. The lecture series was given at Hannover in November and December 1923, and at Nordhausen (Saxony) in January 1924.

On page 85 in *How Can Men Fight Mammon?*, "transvaluation of all values" is a phrase from Nietzche's *The Antichrist*.

For Bible reference for *How Can Men Fight Mammon?*, see: 1 Corinthians 2.7; 2 Corinthians 3.14; 4.4; 1 Corinthians 2.10-12; Galatians 4.8-9; John 8.44; Matthew 12.43-45; Mark 5.6 ff.; John 12.31; 16.8-11; Luke 16.9; Matthew 22.21; Luke 6.24-25; Matthew 19.21; 26.64; Acts 1.9-14; 2.1-4; 2.42-47; 4.32-37; Mark 9.40; Luke 9.50; Matthew 12.30; Luke 11.23; Matthew 9.38; James 5.1-7.

God Mammon and the Living God is based on Eberhard Arnold's own revision of the text of *Der Gott Mammon*, a lecture he gave on October 18, 1924, in the small mining town of Lichtenstein in Saxony, before a predominantly working class audience who were mostly hostile to the Christianity of the organized churches. In 1939 an English version appeared as a paperback under the title, *God and Anti-God* (Plough Publishing House).

The words from Zoroaster are translated from the book by Paul Eberhardt, *Das Rufen des Zarathushtra (Die Gathas des Awesta), Ein Versuch ihren Sinn zu geben*, Eugen Diederichs, Jena, 1913. Pages 15-18, 11-14.

For Bible reference see: 2 Corinthians 4.4; Revelation 2.24; Luke 13.10-17; Ephesians 2.1-2; John 8.44; Mark 5.8; Luke 16.9.

The Decision — see *How Can Men Fight Mammon?* above. The story referred to in *The Empress' Poor Sister,* is the story of Wassili Ossipowitsch Rachoff (1863-ca.1905).

For Bible reference see: 2 Corinthians 4.4; John 12.31; 14.30; 16.11; Matthew 19.16-26; Romans 7.14.

Resistance by Surrender is the title supplied here for a group of short passages selected and translated from the book, *Innenland,* by Eberhard Arnold. More about *Innenland* is to be found in *When the Time Was Fulfilled* (Plough Publishing House, 1965), pages 211-213.

The Spirit of Life Overcomes was translated for the present book from the transcript of a talk on October 22, 1933, in a meeting at the Rhön Bruderhof. At this time, under the Hitler government, there was already increasing hostility and danger to the Bruderhof community and what it stood for.

For Bible reference see: Matthew 6.22.

Present Experience — *Future Kingdom* was an article published in *Das Neue Werk* in 1919, entitled *Das Gegenwartserlebnis des Zukunft-reiches*. This is its first publication in English.

Eberhard Arnold had spoken on the Sermon on the Mount at the Whitsun Conference of the German Christian Student Movement on the Frauenberg Mountain near Marburg, June 13 to 15, 1919. *Present Experience — Future Kingdom* reflects this crucial address which caused a great stir at the time and led to Eberhard Arnold's beginning of full community life in Sannerz in 1920. This Marburg Conference was reported as follows by Erwin Wissman in *Die Furche*: "This was the Sermon on the Mount in the full force of its impact, in its absolute and undiminished relevance, its unconditional absoluteness. Here there was no compromise. Whoever wants to belong to this Kingdom must give himself wholly and go through with it to the last!"

"The future State," a term often used in this chapter, is meant to emphasize that the kingdom of God is a government, a dominion, a state in which God rules over men.

For Bible reference see: Luke 3.11; John 3.6; 3.5; Matthew 5.3; 6.19; 6.24; 7.12; 7.21; Luke 9.55-56; 12.49; 14.26; Matthew 19.16-22; Luke 12.33; Micah 6.8; Luke 14.33; Matthew

25.40; Luke 18.17; Matthew 11.12; Luke 16.16.

God and the Future of Men is a lecture given at the town of Lichtenstein in Saxony in October 1924 and entitled *Gott und die Zukunft der Menschen*. It was the last in the series of five lectures begun with *Der Gott Mammon* (in this volume, *God Mammon and the Living God*). Much that this lecture contained was also used by Eberhard Arnold in guiding his own older children through the story of mankind's history. The words of Zoroaster are translated from *Das Rufen des Zarathushtra (Die Gathas des Awesta), Ein Versuch ihren Sinn zu geben* by Paul Eberhardt, Eugen Diederichs, Jena, 1913.

For Bible reference see: Hosea 10.12; Ezekiel 18.21; 37; Mark 1.15.

The Jesus of the Four Gospels is translated from the transcript of a longer talk in a meeting on May 13, 1934, at the Rhön Bruderhof, most likely given from notes. It is easy to feel in this talk and others how urgently and intensely the words of Jesus were being applied to guide the actual daily life together.

For Bible reference see: Luke 14.28-33; Matthew 23.13-36; Luke 11.42-52; Revelation 20.6.

BOOKS BY THE SAME AUTHOR

Inner Land: A Guide into the Heart and Soul of the Bible

The Early Christians after the Death of the Apostles

Love and Marriage in the Spirit

Seeking for the Kingdom of God: Origins of the Bruderhof Communities

Living Churches: The Essence of Their Life
Vol. 1 *Love to Christ and Love to the Brothers*
Vol. 2 *The Meaning and Power of Prayer Life*

The Heavens Are Opened

When the Time Was Fulfilled by Eberhard Arnold and others

Inner Words for Every Day of the Year by Eberhard Arnold and others

Eberhard Arnold: A Testimony of Church Community from His Life and Writings

Children's Education in Community

Why We Live in Community

OTHER BOOKS FROM THE PLOUGH PUBLISHING HOUSE

Torches Together by Emmy Arnold

In the Image of God: Marriage and Chastity in Christian Life by Heini Arnold

Freedom from Sinful Thoughts by Heini Arnold

Confession of Faith by Peter Rideman

Christoph Blumhardt and His Message by R. Lejeune

Free catalog of Plough books sent on request.